Through the Eyes
of Tiger Cubs

Through the Eyes of Tiger Cubs

Views of Asia's Next Generation

Mark L. Clifford
Janet Pau

WILEY

John Wiley & Sons (Asia) Pte. Ltd.

Other Wiley Editorial Offices
John Wiley & Sons, 111 River Street, Hoboken, NJ 07030, USA
John Wiley & Sons, The Atrium, Southern Gate, Chichester, West Sussex, P019 8SQ,
    United Kingdom
John Wiley & Sons (Canada) Ltd., 5353 Dundas Street West, Suite 400, Toronto, Ontario,
    M9B 6HB, Canada
John Wiley & Sons Australia Ltd., 42 McDougall Street, Milton, Queensland 4064,
    Australia
Wiley-VCH, Boschstrasse 12, D-69469 Weinheim, Germany

Library of Congress Cataloging-in-Publication Data
ISBN 978–1–118–09463–1 (Paperback)
ISBN 978–1–118–09466–2 (ePDF)
ISBN 978–1–118–09465–5 (Mobi)
ISBN 978–1–118–09464–8 (ePub)

Typeset in 11.5/13.5 pts BemboAR by MPS Limited, a Macmillan Company

Printed in Singapore by Markono Print Media Pte. Ltd.
10 9 8 7 6 5 4 3 2 1

Contents

Foreword

The Asian Renaissance: Through Young Asian Eyes

A new historical era has begun. Many call it the *rise* of Asia. But it should be more accurately described as the *return* of Asia. From the year 1 to 1820, China and India consistently provided the world's largest economies. Hence, the last 200 years of European and America domination of world history have been a major historical aberration. And all historical aberrations come to a natural end.

The Asian renaissance that we are witnessing today is therefore a completely natural phenomenon. Yet, despite its naturalness, there is no guarantee that there will be a smooth or easy passage to a new peaceful and prosperous era. Indeed, Asians will have to overcome many major challenges and obstacles.

The generation that will have to deal with these future challenges are the young Asians of today. Despite the important role they will have to play on the world stage, few know how they view the world or how they perceive Asia's future roles and responsibilities. This gap in our knowledge explains why it was timely for the Asia Business

Council, the Lee Kuan Yew School of Public Policy, and *Time* magazine to launch the Asia's Challenge 2020 essay competition in 2010.

This volume of essay extracts can play an important role in developing a better global understanding of Asian thinking. Of course, there is a wide range of perspectives, reflecting the diversity of Asia. At the same time, some common themes emerge. Despite the painful experience of colonialism and imperialism, there is little anger in these essays. Instead, the traditional Asian pragmatic streak comes through. Yes, Asia faces many challenges. But these young Asian writers do believe that these challenges can be overcome.

The essays reveal that young Asians are deeply aware of the major challenges to Asian societies: from demographic changes to educational challenges; from great power rivalries to domestic political challenges; from the environmental impact of Asia's return to the challenges of a growing gap between rich and poor; from the despair of corruption to the hope of technology.

Despite the awareness of these overwhelming challenges, there is also a strong streak of optimism running through many of these essays. At the end of the day, the essay competition winners are confident that Asia will overcome these challenges. Youth from other regions, from Africa to Latin America, from Europe to America, will also benefit from reading these essays.

We at the Lee Kuan Yew School of Public Policy are proud to have co-sponsored the Asia's Challenge 2020 essay competition and we are pleased that much of the hard work put in by the contestants can now be shared worldwide.

Kishore Mahbubani
Dean, Lee Kuan Yew School of Public Policy
National University of Singapore

Acknowledgments

This book is the work of many minds. First, we want to thank the nearly 400 essayists who entered Asia's Challenge 2020. These young Asians took the time to let us know what they thought were the biggest challenges facing the region over the next decade and what should be done about them. From among the many essayists, we want to particularly thank and commend the nearly 100 authors whose writings we drew upon for this book.

Thanks go also to our partners, *Time* magazine and the Lee Kuan Yew School of Public Policy at the National University of Singapore. We owe a special debt to the contest's judges, two from each of the sponsoring organizations, all of whom made important contributions. *Time*'s former deputy managing editor and international editor, Michael Elliott, as well as Asia editor Zoher Abdoolcarim, generously donated their time as judges. Michael has since become president and CEO of the ONE foundation. At the Lee Kuan Yew School, Dean Kishore Mahbubani and Vice Dean Astrid Tuminez served as judges. Kudos to Kishore, who somehow managed to make time in his schedule to write the Foreword. Many others at both *Time* and the Lee Kuan Yew School helped in myriad ways to make the contest a success. Ambassador Tommy Koh's moving speech at the award ceremony held in Singapore in December 2010 and his encouragement helped prompt us to embark on this book project.

At the Asia Business Council, we want to acknowledge the enthusiastic support shown by members, especially by the Board of Trustees, led by former Chairman Qin Xiao and current Chairman Marjorie Yang. Above all, we want to thank trustees Nobuyuki Idei and Lubna Olayan, who served on our judging panel and, along with the other four judges, undertook the time-consuming task of choosing the winning essays.

This project would not have been as comprehensive, as accurate, or as quick to come to fruition were it not for the help of our Asia Business Council colleagues. Council researcher Alex Zhang and Princeton-in-Asia fellow Kari Wilhelm drafted chapters, did much of the underlying research, and took on a great deal of the necessary work involved in a book like this, ranging from sifting through the nearly 400 essays to fact-checking. Publications editor Sheri Prasso pushed us to make this a far more coherent and well-thought-out book than it otherwise would have been.

The Council's administrative director, Winnie Wu, and administrative associate, Bonnie Chang, continue to ensure the Council's smooth day-to-day operations. Their efficiency, grace, and good humor made the task of juggling this book and our other tasks possible.

Rosalie Siegel graciously provided thoughtful counsel in structuring the book contract. At John Wiley & Sons, we want to thank our publisher, Nick Wallwork, for seeing the merits of this project, as well as his colleagues, Jules Yap, Janis Soo, and Todd Tedesco, who helped bring it to fruition.

The usual disclaimers apply: We are responsible for any errors. Much of the essayists' material is, of course, opinionated; throughout, we have tried to make the distinction between fact and opinion clear to readers.

Mark Clifford would like to thank Melissa, Anya, and Ted for their continuing love and support.

Janet Pau would like to thank Jimmy, Jocelyn, Josiah, her parents, Wing Foo and Miranda, and her brother, Alex, for the love and joy they bring into her life.

Hong Kong
August 2011

Introduction

Meet the Tiger Cubs

Over the next decade, a new generation will begin to take over the reins of leadership in Asia. The region they inherit inevitably will be quite different from the one they grew up in. They in turn will bring a leadership style that will be different from that of their elders.

The first half of the twentieth century in Asia was a story of war and continuing poverty punctuated by revolution. The following three decades saw de-colonization and its aftermath, with Japan and the Four Asian Tigers (Hong Kong, Singapore, South Korea, and Taiwan) engaged in a momentous economic transformation. The last 30 years have been a story of high economic growth interrupted by the sharp 1997–98 contraction and the 2008–2009 global financial crisis.

On the whole, Asia has gone through a time of remarkable peace and prosperity. Asians coming into adulthood today have been alive at a time when large-scale armed conflict has been absent from their lives, and when much of the region has witnessed the fastest sustained growth that our planet has ever seen.

Asia's leaders of tomorrow will come from a generation that has known little but good times. What are their worries, and what are their ideas for solving Asia's many challenges?

To help answer these questions, the Asia Business Council joined with *Time* magazine and the Lee Kuan Yew School of Public Policy at the National University of Singapore to organize an essay contest for Asian nationals under the age of 32. It was open to youth from countries stretching from Japan in the east to Saudi Arabia and Turkey in the west—from the Pacific to the Suez Canal and the Bosporus. We followed the lead of the World Bank's program for young professionals in picking an upper age limit that was still young, but was old enough that many of our essayists had finished their studies and had been working for some time.

By opening the contest to those born after 1978—coincidentally, when Deng Xiaoping initiated China's economic reforms—we ensured that we would have Chinese writers who grew up under a reform agenda, and Indians who would have only dim memories of the era before their country's sweeping economic reforms were introduced in 1991. South Korean contestants would have, at most, distant memories of the years when a military dictatorship ruled their country, and most Filipino writers would not remember Ferdinand Marcos, let alone the assassination of the father of current President Benigno Aquino III during Marcos's administration. Japanese contestants would have only childhood memories of the boom years of the 1980s. Each of the writers tackled the challenge of outlining, in 3,000 words or less, what he or she thinks is Asia's biggest challenge over the next decade, why, and what can be done about it.

Young people from 21 countries and economies around Asia submitted 385 valid essays. India had the most submissions, followed by the Philippines. The average age of the essayists was 23. This book, which draws on selected excerpts from the essays as well as broader information, including statistical and anecdotal data, reveals that the concerns of Asia's new generation of young adults fall within two broad categories—Asia's people and Asia as a region.

■ ■ ■

Nowhere in history have more young people been catapulted into the modern world with the speed and intensity of today's young Asians. Three decades ago the region was poor, far behind the West. Today its cities and schools are emerging as new models. Its broadband speeds and Internet access rates, its high-speed trains and urban train networks, the facilities at many of its new university campuses, and even its soaring property prices in some cases have vaulted Asia ahead of the West. Asia is now a continent of promise and possibility.

The parents of today's young Asians knew hunger and revolution. Now, no longer living in a world defined by poverty, today's young Asians are better-fed and better-educated, and have access to the world through the Internet in a way that would have been unthinkable at the time they were born. Thanks to heavy investments in education, more of them can go to school and, once there, study for more years than their parents. They can aspire to jobs in areas of biotech, engineering, information technology, and finance that literally did not exist a generation ago.

Many of them grew up in Asia's tiger economies—a term initially referring to the high-performing economies of Hong Kong, Singapore, South Korea, and Taiwan but later more broadly describing economies that are growing rapidly on a sustained basis. They belong to the generation we call *Tiger Cubs*—they have protective parents who often use their newfound affluence to ensure that their children make the most of opportunities that the elder generation never had. And, as everyone from aunts and uncles to teachers and government officials warns these young Asians, they live in a modern jungle. Country competes against country, school competes against school, student competes against student. Resources are scarce, competition fierce, and survival is not guaranteed. Though competition is nothing new, the heightened expectations of the Tiger Cubs and their families make their desire for success that much stronger.

The result is a unique group. Increased economic prosperity, smaller families, and more resources directed to each child have given the Tiger Cubs a view of the world that is both privileged and insecure.

The American and European counterparts of these young Asians— for the purposes of this book, those born from 1978 to the early 1990s—are generally known as Generation Y. This generation, also called the Millennial generation, describes a demographic cohort that is mostly comprised of children of the Baby Boomers, the generation born after World War II. In the United States, members of Generation Y are generally seen as digitally savvy, culturally liberal, and privileged as compared to their parents. They are also sometimes called the "Peter Pan" or "boomberang" generation, because of the perception that many 20-somethings delay or prolong their paths to adulthood after graduating from university.

The Tiger Cub generation, or Asia's Generation Y, has a population of almost 1.5 billion and shares some of the characteristics, both positive and negative, with its Western counterpart.[1]

In mainland China, children of one-child families growing up in cities and enjoying the undivided attention of their parents are called *balinghou* ("post-80") or "little emperors." They are seen as optimistic about the future, individualistic, and concerned with material comforts. *Time* calls them the "Me generation"—they are self-interested, pragmatic, and materialistic.[2]

Those born in Hong Kong in the 1980s also are called the "post-80" generation. Commentators ascribe a range of conflicting characteristics to them: They are activist and entrepreneurial, yet they are also said to be overindulged, lacking in adaptive capabilities, not committed to regular work, and overly critical of the government and business establishment.

Young Indians are described as being "in a hurry." They are impatient to graduate and in a rush to take advantage of job opportunities that have arisen from the country's IT services boom. They look for jobs that pay well and enable them to buy things quickly without saving for years.

In Japan, young males are called the *soshoku danshi*, or "herbivore generation." In contrast with the previous generation, who were seen as stereotypical corporate warriors and workaholic salary-men, these young men are seen as uncompetitive, uncommitted to work, and dependent on their parents. Men and women in their twenties who still live with their parents rather than independently are sometimes called *parasaito shinguru*, or "parasite singles." Freelance or unemployed workers are called "freeters." Along similar lines, in Taiwan, members of the "strawberry generation" are easily bruised and cannot withstand social pressures.

Twenty-somethings in South Korea are called the "post-386" generation. The "386" generation, a play on the popular computer model of the era, referred to youths who were in their thirties as they led the pro-democracy movement during the 1980s. By contrast, the post-386s are more concerned about the increased competition for jobs and high levels of youth unemployment than about politics. Another nickname for this group is the "880,000 won" generation, referring to those who have worked hard and achieved at school but are trapped in low-paying, temporary, or contract jobs with a monthly salary around this figure (about $650).

While no doubt generalizations, these labels provide a glimpse of the opportunities these young Asians are presented with as well as perceptions of their preparedness for the future.

Many of the Tiger Cubs have grown up in the midst of the so-called Asian miracle, though the word miracle doesn't capture the sheer grit and determination of hundreds of millions of people, notably in their parents' and grandparents' generations, to better their lives. The economic transformation of Asia has meant dramatic improvements in living standards. In the 30 years from 1975 to 2005, the high-performing U.S. economy grew its GDP per person fivefold. Singapore, Hong Kong, and South Korea, while starting out at a lower base, each grew theirs more than 10 times.[3]

This new generation has come of age at a time when Asia and the world have undergone dramatic transitions. Its members live in an Asia that has embraced globalization, and, thanks to free trade, has been one of the biggest beneficiaries of it. Yet Asia is seeing the system come under strain, as young people who have been brought up during prosperous times and are taught to be optimistic about the future are confronted with brutal realities as Asia faces new challenges.

Asia in 2020

Asia holds an extraordinary potential for continued economic growth and progress, with growth in GDP, wages, and spending power expected to outpace the West in the decade ahead. A study from the Economist Intelligence Unit (EIU) estimates Asia's share of the world economy will increase from 35 percent in 2005 to 43 percent in 2020. China is expected to become the world's second-largest consumer market, and the size of India's consumer market is expected to rival Europe's by 2020. China will send more tourists abroad than any other country. The majority of new jobs will come from developing Asia, with India alone making up 30 percent of the net increase in global employment. The share of households with annual disposable incomes of $5,000 to $15,000 is expected to grow from about one-third to about one-half of all households in both China and Indonesia in 2020, and from 15 percent to 41 percent in India.[4]

However, the next decade is filled with a new set of challenges for the region—perhaps we can call them "mid-life challenges." Asia's rise faces many obstacles, as problems created from environmental neglect, the continent's growing and aging population, and unbalanced growth become more prevalent. The increasing needs of Asia's population, which is expected to reach 4.6 billion by 2020, will lead to pressure on food, water, and energy resources.[5] Under a business-as-usual scenario, in the next 20 years, Asia's overall demand for water will exceed supply by 40 percent.[6] Meanwhile, a shift in the demographic makeup of Asia's people—Asia will house 588 million people over age 60 by 2020, up from 414 million in 2010—will increase the region's need for healthcare and social security.[7] Some of Asia's many simmering conflicts have worsened in the past decade as a result of the September 11, 2001 terrorist attacks and the Afghan and Iraq wars that followed. Compounding these issues is the ominous shadow of climate change, the effects of which could further jeopardize Asia's food supply. The region's pollution—already the highest in the world—is expected to worsen in the coming decade, leading to increased health problems among Asians. In a region where such major challenges are pushing in from all sides, continued growth is far from guaranteed.

Besides threatening to stunt Asia's growth, these challenges, in a gloomy scenario, could destabilize the region. As evidenced by the youth-led uprisings in the Middle East and North Africa, young populations have sparked unprecedented changes to governments and societies. The 2011 Arab Awakening was in part triggered by dissatisfaction with the ruling regimes and joblessness among youth. Although the rest of Asia hasn't seen anything like the tumult of the Arab world, young Asians are concerned about problems that have been neglected as a result of an excessive focus on economic growth.

There are some signs that this generation may be the most protest-prone of any since the 1970s and 1980s. In 2005, South Korean students protested the high competitiveness of the education system, the first demonstration against education policies in memory.[8] Post-80 protestors in Hong Kong staged lengthy and disruptive protests against the government's plans to demolish the Star Ferry Pier and Queen's Pier in 2006 and 2007, respectively, and to build a high-speed rail into mainland China in 2010, opposing the lack of a democratic discussion leading up to the decisions. Also in 2010, Filipino students pressed President Aquino to improve the quality of education following announcements of budget cuts in the educational system.[9]

Despite the rosy pictures of macroeconomic growth, many of the Tiger Cubs are uncertain that they will have better lives than their parents. They are increasingly looking for change. They distrust those currently in power and question their leaders' abilities to address longer-term economic and social issues. They can get organized to make their dissent known and make change happen. As one of the essayists, Poh Wei Leong, 29, Singapore, writes:

> Let's face it. The world is going to be increasingly populated, run, and led by Generation Y. Much as their attitudes towards work and life may be antithetical to those of the Baby Boomers, brushing them aside is akin to ignoring those people who build our future. They add more diversity in terms of viewpoints, ideas, and values, and are not keeping mum about it, at least in the blogosphere. Most importantly, many of the Generation Y Asians have parents who have lived under a different political era, and this allows them to witness firsthand whether they want to grow up to be like their parents, and whether they want their world to be the same as their parents'.

His sentiments may be indicative of broader views of young Singaporean voters, who in the country's May 2011 general elections helped the opposition party win an unprecedented share of the vote. Young Singaporeans used online forums to rally support for opposition candidates.

The Tiger Cubs have a growing recognition that they must work to solve national and regional challenges. Those paying the price of inaction will not be the people in positions of power today. Instead, it will be them.

This book aims to present Asia's challenges, and their proposed solutions, as seen through the eyes of these Tiger Cubs. The first set of challenges involves issues with Asia's people. While school enrollment has improved, the education system remains deficient. Despite high growth, many people are left behind. Growing populations in already-populous countries strain governments and families, as does increasing agedness.

The second set of challenges involves Asia as a region. The physical environment is under great stress due not only to large populations and increased consumption but also to natural disasters. Governance is often corrupt and inefficient. Disputes between countries occasionally flare up. Asia as a region does not have a clear and common identity. Each of these challenges will be addressed in the book's chapters.

By understanding the worries, ideas, and visions of the nearly 100 young Asians whose writing is excerpted in this book, we hope to give a better picture of those who will be at the helm of an Asia that is working hard to sustain its growth in challenging times ahead. How effectively will the Tiger Cubs be able to lead Asia in the future? The answer depends not just on whether they will be given opportunities and resources to do so, but whether they will seize the challenges ahead. The first step, however, is to give them a platform so that they can gain the confidence required to move their countries forward. The Asia's Challenge 2020 essay contest and this book are a place for Asia's Tiger Cub generation to find its voice.

Part I

ASIA'S PEOPLE

Chapter 1

Education

Thousands of people are forcing themselves across a narrow footbridge.

—*Chinese proverb*

Introduction

The reaction in the United States to 15-year-old Shanghai students besting Americans in reading, math, and science, was shock. President Barack Obama, responding to news of the Program for International Student Assessment (PISA) test results released in December 2010, declared "our generation's Sputnik moment is back," promising that this would galvanize a far-reaching U.S. response similar to that which followed the 1957 Soviet Sputnik satellite launch.[1]

Yes, test scores in Shanghai, and in South Korea and Singapore, rank among the highest in the world. But where Obama sees an unstoppable

11

juggernaut, Asia's Tiger Cubs see all-too-closely the many problems of Asia's schooling. Most Asian schools are focused on stuffing students' heads with facts. The notion of producing critical thinkers, of making students learners for life rather than masters of a defined body of factual knowledge, has been slow to come to Asia. There is recognition that China, and indeed much of Asia, has a long way to go in winning this space race of education when it comes to issues of quality rather than test scores. Despite recent years of economic growth, the education system is archaic.

A strong, forward-thinking education system is important because today's students are tomorrow's citizens. Today's Tiger Cubs are tomorrow's leaders. Today's Generation Y-ers are the ones who will create the jobs and wealth needed for continued economic growth, the ones who will provide the leadership needed for national excellence.

Asia has done an extraordinary job of boosting literacy and expanding educational opportunities in recent decades. An increasing share of young people in Asia receive basic education, with secondary enrollment rates increasing more than 10 percentage points between 2000 and 2010.[2] Students' school life expectancy, or the years of education they receive, has increased by 1.5 years on average.[3] Tertiary enrollment rates, while lagging behind those of many Western countries, have also seen a large jump. Perhaps most important of all, more girls are going to school, although too many still don't.

Asia's large population means a huge supply of potential future workers. The world's working-age population (those aged 15–59) will grow from 4.3 billion in 2010 to 4.7 billion in 2020, with Asia accounting for about 62 percent of the total, or 2.9 billion people. While some economies, including China, Japan, Hong Kong, South Korea, and Taiwan, face an aging population problem and will see an absolute decline in working-age populations by 2020, developing Asian economies, including India, Indonesia, Pakistan, the Philippines, Vietnam, Saudi Arabia, and Malaysia, will see labor force increases, making them relatively labor-rich. Singapore and Thailand will face an aging population but still make modest gains in the size of working-age populations.[4]

The growing working-age population of Asia could be a huge asset for the region if it is translated into productive labor for existing and new industries. But the enormous pool of human talent will be wasted absent dramatic improvements in education. On both a moral and practical level, policy makers need to do more to ensure better education. Despite dramatic improvements in recent decades, nearly half of Bangladeshis and Pakistanis and one-third of Indians are illiterate.[5] According to UN statistics, almost half the women and one-third of men in South Asia have no formal education.[6] Here the task is not a Sputnik race, but the basics of reading and writing and the ability to do simple sums. A pessimistic World Bank report notes that, with the exception of the Maldives, "no South Asian nation is currently upgrading the skill of its population at a speed that will allow it to catch up with East Asia and the rest of the world over the medium term. Some indications even suggest that the gaps relative to some East Asian competitor countries may be widening rather than closing."[7]

For those who go through the education system, the transition to the job market often is rocky. In 2009, more than six million college graduates in China were seeking jobs, including one million who graduated the previous year but were still jobless. According to a survey of human-resources professionals in China in 2005 by McKinsey & Company, a global consulting firm, less than 10 percent of the graduates from Chinese universities are hirable by multinational companies, due to the lack of practical experience, as well as poor English and communication skills.[8]

At the basic level, young Asian essayists are concerned about certain groups of people not receiving formal education, in particular, the rural poor and girls. Without schooling, they will not have the opportunity to live better lives. In addition, the Tiger Cubs who have gone through their countries' education systems lament that there is an overemphasis on rote learning and a lack of emphasis on creativity and workplace skills. At the end of the formal schooling process, many worry about the uncertain future. Their sentiments reflect the difficult task that education systems have, as many of Asia's economies transition into postindustrial societies that require workers to produce ideas rather than basic manufactured goods.

Young Asians who are products of their respective countries' education systems agree that the region's grand goal should be to improve its workforce quality. As Danica Elaine Ang, 22, the Philippines, puts it:

> As a key to human capital development, education is deemed to enhance individuals' income levels and social participation. Education enhances language, technical, and social skills that are significant in enhancing the viability of socio-economic integration and intergenerational income gains. Low literacy rates, as an indicator of low human capital, have spillover effects such as low research and development (R&D), and in some instances low foreign direct investment (FDI).

But in order to yield these benefits, a number of big challenges, both in the education system and the job market that graduates eventually enter, need to be overcome. The World Bank is not confident that South Asia's policy makers fully understand the role of education in economic growth:

> What is not yet clear, however, is whether governments are as yet fully aware of the crucial importance of education and training policies for sustaining the current high rates of growth in the region, and whether such policies feature prominently in relation to other national priorities on governments' agendas.[9]

Education Access

The first problem of concern for young Asians is unequal opportunities for education for different population groups, mainly those living in poorer areas, and girls. Large populations of rural children are not enrolled in school, compared to their urban counterparts. Girls have traditionally had fewer educational opportunities than boys. The results are illiteracy as well as economic losses for countries.

Regional inequality mainly hurts rural populations who are too poor to go to school. "The average fee for primary school in Asia is approximately $4.40 (per month), which rural people in some countries find impossible to afford, so a reduction in the fee amount can usher in more children from this sector," says Ashwin Menon, 20, India.

Observes Karishma Singh Ahluwalia, 31, India, a teacher:

Children of low-income parents have to brave both the scorching summer of the subcontinent, and the cold winter, without air conditioners, heaters, and many times even blankets. These are the young generations out there who can sense the change, and are weary of it just like they are weary of most things in their lives. They laugh and play just like the other children, and dance and sing, but deep down inside, they know that they are different; they know that they do not have the same opportunities. They are aware of this. They live with it every day. Are things changing? What do I tell them? Why isn't the promise of globalization enough for them? Because they will never get there. They do not have the education. In the subcontinent, the public school system has largely failed, and NGOs mostly engage in semi-formal education, to give these children something to do and to teach them basic life skills. Those who go to these public schools seldom make it to college. Those who don't get enrolled in open schools instead, which only give you the curriculum and no teaching aid, thereby rendering them largely ineffective.

There is a strong (and well-founded) belief that better schooling equips youngsters for non-farm jobs that earn better incomes, and that education helps overcome a whole host of problems. Avish Acharya, 19, Nepal, writes:

Today, people are more and more becoming aware of the necessity of education and are sending their children, who otherwise worked on farms all day, to schools. I have a positive belief that once the majority of the population in the village is educated, the situation will improve. An educated population would elect capable lawmakers and would ensure the region is not deprived of development. If the entire nation has a similar story, political stability is sure to follow. Political stability encourages investment and trade, which further increases employment. Educated citizens press for more transparency and accountability. Educated citizens also understand that the

environment must be protected, and hence will try to ensure
that development will not be uncontrolled and unmanaged.
Of all challenges, education is the driving force that can trigger
positive growth and help overcome most problems. A well-
educated and hence skilled human resource is the most powerful
asset a nation can hope to achieve. They can improve politics,
the economy, trade, and research. Asia faces the challenge of
developing its human power.

Similarly, Aprakrita Shankar Narayanan, 16, India, writes:

The benefits of a free market would come in the future for
Asia only if all the populace has equal access to opportunity.
It is vitally important that every child gets access to primary
education, and, based on ability, has the opportunity to progress to his or her full potential. In India recently there has been
a notification that every school in the country should accept
25 percent of its students from the economically weaker sections
of society. This may not be the perfect solution. But it is in the
right direction. Gifted children should have the opportunity
to go to exclusive schools regardless of the economic status of
their parents. This is vital for building a vibrant, wealthy, and
inclusive society. The IIT entrance exam is one of the fairest
and [most] objective methods of admitting students. Entry to
any of the Indian Institutes of Technology is solely on the basis
of the entrance exam, and there is no subjective element to it.
As a capitalist society produces winners and losers, it is vital
that the system is seen as fair. It is cronyism and anti-competitive
practices that give free markets a bad name.

While many Asian governments and organizations are already making efforts in improving education, young Asians lament that resources
for rural areas are lacking. They suggest that both the government and
private sector step in. First, governments can encourage private investments to focus less on urban and more on rural areas. Acharya notes:

Urbanization, when unplanned and unmanaged, leads to the
disparity between two places. Employment and development

gets concentrated only in certain areas. To overcome this challenge, the government must encourage investments in backward areas by cooperating with the private sector. Attractive tax exemptions and capital funding could be two ways of encouraging the investors towards the rural areas.

Second, well-organized teaching programs drawing on talented students and graduates can be used to recruit passionate and qualified teachers to work at rural schools. Says Menon, who cites the Teach for India program:

Governments should establish more educational institutions in villages, and if the problem of finding tutors arises, the answer would be to send trainees and interns who aspire to become teachers to these places. This will not only gear them for a future of imparting knowledge, but will also educate people in the countryside, and, so, we kill two birds with one stone. [Teach for India] involves encouraging professionals in various fields to spend at least one third of their time educating the underprivileged. In Pakistan and Afghanistan, the [very high] illiteracy rates can be reduced to around 10 percent in the next four to five years by forming societies similar to Teach for India across Asia. A monthly stipend can perhaps be used as an incentive for educated people to commit to these organizations since many Asian employees are paid meager salaries.

Mariyam Thomas, 25, India, suggests a voluntary program. She points out that such programs are currently less organized and valued in Asia than in developed countries in Europe:

A voluntary program could create an exchange of skills and knowledge, within schools, colleges and universities. . . . For example, Rishi Valley School, part of the Krishnamurti Foundation located in Andhra Pradesh, provides a rural education center for local children living in the nearby villages. Students at the age of 16 to 18 years, as part of the schools' curriculum and activities, have to teach an English class to the rural kids. At a college/university level, volunteering with non-governmental organizations (NGOs) and charities in whatever capacity can provide insight and practicality to one's education. For example, there are international programs such as Engineers Without Borders and Doctors Without Borders where engineering and medical students can use their experience to provide sustainable solutions to solve critical problems faced by disadvantaged communities around the world. This not only helps improve living conditions and contributes positively to communities, but also provides practical implementation of the technical skills and basic education they gained in university.

Governments can also collaborate with NGOs to develop teachers and leaders who are focused on lowering inequalities in education. Says Kamanasish Sen, 26, India:

These agencies would collaborate with the government and the local administration so that they have adequate support from the government. The mission of the agencies should be to create leaders who would work to lower inequality in education in the countries. The education leaders would be placed by the agencies in different schools, mostly government and low-income schools in the respective areas. They would teach in the school for a certain span of time (say two years). Education leaders would be assigned different classes individually, and they would be in charge of them for the entire span of teaching. The difference between the education leaders and the normal teachers would be in the commitment and engagement levels of the education leaders.

Fixing problems with teachers in less-developed regions greatly improves the effectiveness of education. Tan Zi Xiang, 16, Singapore, believes teacher absenteeism needs to be addressed:

Teacher absenteeism is another patent flaw of some education systems in Asia. A study by a team of economists (Kremer, Muralidharan, Chaudhury, Hammer and Rogers) from Harvard and the World Bank found that at any random time, 25 percent of the teachers in central and northern India are absent from school. In a country where, according to a *BusinessWeek* article in May 2004, 97 percent of education spending goes to teacher salaries, this cannot be ignored.

Benjamin Joshua Ong, 20, Singapore, points out issues with teacher qualifications:

A number of teachers do not see the importance of their jobs. Others lack training: Less than half of Cambodia's lower and upper secondary school teachers are considered to be "qualified" for their jobs. This has a negative impact on students, who tend to learn by example.

Technology also offers promise in breaking down the distance barrier encountered by rural schools. Ong writes:

Physical structure aside, information and communications technology (ICT) infrastructure deserves special attention as a particular tool that can add significant value while reducing long-term costs. A simple computer such as the XO-1 (developed under the One Laptop per Child project) lasts longer than a textbook; has a lower long-term cost (which is otherwise borne by students) as new content can be distributed electronically; and, given the role of ICT in the developed world, provides skills that can enable upward mobility. More significantly, computers can, to an extent, help overcome physical barriers to education by facilitating distance learning.

Likewise, Thomas advocates the use of e-learning for rural schools that "woefully lack basic infrastructure like libraries, playgrounds, labs, even classrooms. These inadequacies can be bridged with computer technology as a teaching tool."

Ong also believes that, ultimately, local communities must be involved:

The solution is for countries to make organized efforts to engage with communities and schools directly. Village officials such as *panchayats* (local governments), Members of Parliament, school principals, and other low-level leaders already have established authority; they just have to be asked to pay attention to the role of education in the context of their local communities. . . . It is very important that the solutions developed in consultation with people and communities consist of more than governments simply throwing money at problems. Indeed, flexibility in the implementation of policy can often be more important than funding, particularly when the people who need help are in the minority.

Regarding the problem of unequal opportunity for women, according to UNESCO, two-thirds of the estimated 793 million illiterate adults in the world are female.[10] "Among minors, the data reveal that 110 million of them are illiterate with 56 percent of them being girls. . . . Countries like India, Pakistan and Afghanistan show high illiteracy amongst women in the rural areas," writes Menon.

Part of the problem, according to Lưu Ngọc Thảo, 17, Vietnam, is the "Eastern culture of male preference. Discrimination against girls occurs in both pre-natal and post-natal periods, leading to deterioration in living environments for women and lower social status."

Frederick A. Halcon, 31, the Philippines, a young professor, talks about his own family history:

I remember hearing stories that my only aunt from my paternal grandparents never went on to finish her schooling simply because she was expected to do household chores, unlike my father and his brothers who were able to earn their college diplomas.

He goes on to cite research supporting the belief that "educating women produces greater results since students tend to delay marriage, raise fewer but healthier offspring, and to seek employment opportunities that contribute to national productivity." These women, many of whom eventually become mothers, "contribute to the multiplier effects experienced by a nation, particularly on the quality of its human resources for several generations. Thus, it is safe to state that educating a woman improves the state of health and education for herself and her offspring at the grassroots level."

Adds Tan:

For a start, traditional gender roles of females often run contrary to the ideal of an egalitarian education. . . . The need to right these wrongs is more than for the sake of justice and equality; it is argued that more educated women usually have more autonomy in their marital relationships, which contributes to family planning and combating overpopulation.

Both better education and empowerment are key to improving women's opportunities. The first strategy is providing free education for women or reserving seats in colleges for women, "to increase the quality of education in the rural areas and make education mandatory," writes Menon, who continues:

The state of Kerala in India, which has the [most balanced] sex ratio in the country, has already achieved a 100 percent literacy count. Providing free education and reservation of seats for women in colleges is one of the possible solutions, which are already underway in many parts of the continent.

The second strategy is developing curricula and teaching materials with girls in mind. Halcon comments:

One striking realization is that gender considerations should also be made in developing curricula and teaching/learning materials in schools. . . . Society is also encouraged to provide leadership training and infrastructural enhancements that protect the educational interests of women. . . . It is also recommended that gender stereotyping in terms of academic streaming be ended as well. As a classic example, males are to be trained in science and technology while females are expected to be well-versed in the arts and humanities.

Halcon also argues for empowerment of women through education about business and entrepreneurship and provides the example of the University of Asia and the Pacific, which, together with Instituto de Estudios Superiores de la Empresa, the graduate school arm of the University of Navarra in Spain, launched the "10,000 Women Business Training Program" in the Philippines.

There is also a realization that unequal opportunities for rural dwellers and women are indicative of the need to combat more deep-seated cultural and social attitudes, beyond implementing policies focused on education itself. Ong writes:

> Although it is nearly impossible for cultural changes to be made top-down, it is important to note that a key factor behind resistance to cultural change is the perceived foreignness of new culture. While anti-Western tendencies are hardly as strong as they were in the past few decades, Asian states are still likely to be more willing to accept assistance from other Asian countries, which can be in a better position to give relevant, useful advice due to contextual similarities.

To address some of the problems of access, governments need to enforce compulsory education. Acharya writes:

> To begin developing the education sector, the law should enforce compulsory education at least up to the secondary level. Social awareness must be raised about the necessity of education. Education should be accessible to all. A big setback could be regional disparity. Taking into consideration the rural sector of Nepal, the schools here lack the proper infrastructure, libraries, and even trained teachers.

Education Quality

Beyond the problem of education access, young Asians are also concerned about the quality of their countries' educational curricula. Sen, of India, writes about employment challenges facing university graduates in Thailand, Indonesia, China, and India:

> The problem lies in the quality of workers. Employers find that the skill sets they possess are insufficient. The stress on too much tertiary education has just focused on quantity and not on quality, which resulted in useless and redundant curricula in colleges. Employers have been seeking people with *soft skills* such as team-building, effective communication, and also familiarity with computers.

Asian youth blame their early educations, as Sen points out:

> The rote system of education stems from primary education where the only stress is on memorization or grades and abysmally less on learning. This continues in even the higher levels of education where less emphasis is put on class discussions.

Menon, of India, agrees:

> The current system in most nations involves rote recitation and does not, in any way, encourage creative thinking. Creative thinking and emphasis on the liberal arts are what most schools and colleges in Europe and America promote, which gives rise to the all-around development of a student. If we can, somehow, incorporate this learning procedure into Asian education, it will result in a tremendous boost in the capability and potential of students.

This sentiment appears to be widely shared. In reaction to the PISA country rankings mentioned at the beginning of the chapter, China's top rank sparked negative sentiments in the news media and the Internet community, with commentators pointing out the damage to students' health and motivation caused by excessive focus on test preparation, as well as Chinese students' lack of critical-thinking skills and creativity.

What is the result of a lack of creativity? Young Asians worry that it has ramifications for their careers. Chandan Kumar, 28, India, cites himself as an example:

> I am an engineer; I spent four years of engineering to learn the latest technologies, but I have never spent a single day in developing a new technology or an engineering field itself. Like me, thousands of engineers are graduating from college who are no more than good skilled laborers.

Farooq Jamil Alvi, 29, Pakistan, uses Singapore to illustrate:

> The Singapore government has invested heavily in providing early-stage funding to start-ups as well as access to facilities and resources. However, the local populace does not bite. Even

Minister Mentor Lee Kuan Yew addressed this notion. "We have to start experimenting," Lee insists. "The easy things—just getting a blank mind to take in knowledge and become trainable—we have done. Now comes the difficult part. To get literate and numerate minds to be more innovative, to be more productive, that's not easy. It requires a mind-set change, a different set of values." In 2001, a study of entrepreneurial activity in the world's top 29 economies concluded that Singapore remained one of the least entrepreneurial societies in the developed world.

To be sure, some top Asian universities are becoming globally competitive and incorporating a focus on innovation and creativity into their curricula. Menon writes of the prestigious Indian Institutes of Technology (IIT):

However, these universities are few and far between. Most Asian colleges lack the infrastructure to meet these standards. The entrance examinations for these colleges, like the annual Chinese *gaokao* examination or the IIT-JEE examination, are grueling and require months of toil. The IITs are the best technical institutes in India, but besides them, India has very little to offer in terms of top-notch colleges, and most of the other institutes are mediocre in a global rating.

In fact, fewer than 10,000 students enter the IITs each year out of 320,000 who take the entrance exam—a lower matriculation rate than at the top Ivy League universities in the United States. Millions of Indian students graduate each year, but employers complain about the graduates' lack of workplace and innovation skills.[11]

Another writer, Yassif Nagim, 29, Malaysia, laments a culture of conformity that leads to students taking up traditional professions rather than becoming innovative entrepreneurs:

The heart of Asia's dilemma is its culture and values. From the Middle East to Japan, Asia's culture forces its citizens to conform to social norms. In Japan, a strong work ethic with respect to elders is a norm that rarely allows its citizens to challenge the old order. . . . On a micro level, it is common in Asia that students are encouraged to study to become a doctor, lawyer, or accountant. These professions are perceived as respectable, with incomes that should be able to support families. . . . If one were to contrast this with Western countries, their cultures and values are less rigid, and thus the population tends toward individuality. This may lead to more originality in creative thinking. This is not to say that Asia does not have individuals who are innovative. These individuals may be statistical outliers.

Besides government involvement and investment, private-sector resources and expertise can also help improve education quality. Ang, of the Philippines, writes:

Development in human capital can be achieved through national governments' ability to engage in partnerships with private foreign investors in R&D, technological innovation, and training. In order to facilitate a harmonious relationship between governments and firms, national governments must provide the necessary resources and sufficient incentives to encourage private firms to impart education, skills, and training that would meet the ever-changing industry demand.

Public involvement in private universities would keep standards in check. Kumar, of India, writes:

Creating public-private partnerships in existing government universities would yield better results than permitting the growth of private universities where quality is often compromised. Also, a private university is more of a degree-selling corporate [entity] which has to show its growth prospects to its stakeholders. However, in a public-private partnership model, the government may provide much-needed regulation and check the capitalistic tendencies of the education system. In a public-private partnership model, both the university and the corporate [entity] can leverage one another's resources and benefit from one another. Further, royalty and patent obligations could also be rationally worked out between the private entity and the university.

Employing innovative technologies and new methods can help train students. Halcon, of the Philippines, writes:

Being a college educator for a decade now, specializing in the fields of mathematics, management, and economics, I firmly and staunchly believe that investments in innovative education, particularly in business, can play a crucial role in a country's economic development, now that there is empirical evidence suggesting that capital accumulation cannot sustain economic growth alone, that the same has to be coupled with technological progress. . . . To wit, most students, if not all of them, are very much familiar with the traditional way of learning through the lecture method. Now, there are various teaching methodologies and strategies available to them with the aid of information and computer technology. Business students are now familiar with the case method, and they are also encouraged to undergo an internship or on-the-job training before earning their college diplomas. Most business programs, specifically in entrepreneurship, give their students the chance to prepare and execute business plans—complete with financial marketing and production studies. They even have to evaluate the results of their operations.

A focus on more innovation and creativity and an emphasis on critical thinking over memorization have emerged as clear goals in a global race for better education quality. Certainly, young Asians see these as priorities. Their sentiments are perhaps in line with a backlash against the controversial book by Chinese-American author Amy Chua, a self-labeled "Tiger Mother," who made a case for Asian-style parenting that emphasizes discipline and rote learning. The latter is not entirely without merit, however. After all, without learning basic math and science formulas, one may have difficulty creating the next breakthrough technology.

Future Career

For those young Asians who have gone through the education system or are about to complete their studies, what awaits them at the other end is of great concern. Will there be jobs? Will these jobs be decent ones? In Southeast Asia, the International Labor Organization estimates that young people ages 15 to 24 are almost five times more likely to be unemployed than those over 25—the worst ratio in the world. Almost half of the world's unemployed youth, or more than 36 million, live in Asia.[12] Even in China, where the economy has been red-hot, many college graduates in large cities have had trouble finding jobs. Termed the "ant group" or "ant tribe," these graduates typically come from inland provinces and have worked hard to get through the education system, but have trouble finding decent-paying jobs as the supply of college graduates exceed cities' demand for educated talent. Communities of these young people live in cramped quarters in marginal areas on the outskirts of cities.[13]

Unemployment, or underemployment, of educated young Asians appears to be the new reality. Graeco Paul Antipasado, 25, the Philippines, observes that "the crisis environment has certainly had an impact on confidence of younger workers." He cites the falling youth labor force participation rate in a 2010 report by the International Labor Organization (ILO). In East Asia, for example, the participation rate was 67 percent in 2000, but, 10 years later, the same figure stands at 59 percent. Whereas growing educational enrollment is partially responsible for this falling number, the ILO points out the persistent and damaging trend of discouraged workers—those who do not have available job prospects and have given up looking. These young people often have a difficult time reintegrating into the workforce later.[14] Antipasado continues:

> Recent global and regional youth unemployment figures appear to be pointing to the possibility of another "Lost Generation." . . . Beyond numbers, according to the same report young people are prone to working in abysmal conditions. So when young people find jobs, they are often forced to work longer hours under informal, intermittent, and insecure work arrangements.

At the same time that many university graduates are unable to find jobs that match their qualifications, some Asian countries are experiencing a seemingly contradictory trend of brain drain as their top graduates migrate to other countries. This phenomenon occurs particularly in countries where industries requiring educated talent are underdeveloped. In earlier decades, Taiwan, India, and China all experienced a brain drain. Economic growth and industrial development allowed these countries to re-attract some of the migrated talent. Now, worries about the brain drain are surfacing again.

Jeremy Lim, 18, Malaysia, cites some indicative statistics:

> The United Nations Development Program estimated that India loses $2 billion a year due to the emigration of computer experts to the United States. Within the 18 months since January 2008, 300,000 Malaysians migrated overseas and 200,000 of them in the first eight months of 2009. Philippine Airlines lost more than 80 pilots [between 2003 and 2005], comprising 20 percent of their total number. In the past 10 years, out of the almost 200,000 trained nurses in the Philippines, 85 percent are working overseas. Even Singapore, a strong and stable economy, is not immune to the brain drain phenomenon. Estimates of about 1,000 skilled youths [a year] leave the country to seek a better life abroad.

The climate in their home countries, including political instability or a lack of educational or job opportunities, is to blame. Lim continues:

> Though many blame the more attractive West as the main cause of this mass exodus, there are internal factors to consider, such as political turmoil and ongoing conflicts which are prevalent in many countries across Asia. . . . The West still appears to have more opportunities even in these hard times. Asians have often been thought of as practical above other things, and this is seen in the policy of many countries. Courses that are relatively new, as well as courses that are deemed impractical, are rarely or not at all offered in tertiary education institutions. Most governments would not be willing to spend a large amount of funding on courses that appear to have no benefits. Individuals who aspire to take on [certain] fields would have to go to the West where their interests will be better nurtured.

Brain drain is also occurring at the lower end of the labor skill spectrum. Acharya, of Nepal, says:

The biggest challenge in Nepal is to shift people from the agriculture sector to either the manufacturing or the service sector. Thanks to political instability, industries have not been able to flourish. The unemployed manpower that remained had no option but to go to foreign countries to earn money and help their families. Statistics show that around 1,000 people leave Nepal daily to look for work elsewhere.

This may not be an entirely bad thing, however. In the words of Rajiv Gandhi, former prime minister of India, "Better a brain drain than a brain in the drain."[15] Indeed, writes Ang, of the Philippines:

Migration has brought in two seemingly contradictory consequences among developing countries: human capital deficit as effectuated in brain drain, and economic development through remittances. As developing countries lose their skilled and professional labor forces, they are, in return, benefitting from the remittances sent back home by migrants to their families. These remittances affect and improve the countries' GNP and [consumption] that keep the economies of developing countries afloat.

Nonetheless, young Asian writers suggest a two-pronged solution to enhance job creation within countries. Countries need to encourage entrepreneurship among their educated graduates and create migration policies that attract and retain talent. First, governments need to make it easier for young people to start their own businesses.

Acharya points out that creating "ladders" for qualified talent will require practical investments to finance entrepreneurship:

There are people who have sufficient skills and ideas which, when materialized, can create wealth. But, finance is usually a constraint. Commercial banks give loans based on the financial strength of the applicant. Professional qualifications and technical skills usually are ignored. Hence, the government must finance the entrepreneurs. Capital assistance must be provided to skilled entrepreneurs by the government or other financial intermediaries through subsidy. The government must support research in science and technology. Encouraging and providing resources to entrepreneurs comes as a step ahead in mobilizing the human resources of the country. Furthermore, the government can finance programs that aim at training people and developing technical skills.

Second, countries need to improve quality of life in order to attract returnees and retain talent at home. Ang says:

Indeed, people migrate primarily because they aspire to improve their quality of life. Though mobility is one of the choices that people are free to make, the government should not encourage it and make it as a permanent development policy to ease the problem of poverty, unemployment, and unequal distribution of opportunities. Investment in human capital abroad through migration is beneficial. However, in order for countries not to suffer from the detrimental effects of brain drain, return migration must be encouraged.

Making the local education system more attractive by bringing in international professors or rewarding students for staying in their home countries may also help. Lim, of Malaysia, writes:

Governments should focus on building and equipping public universities with facilities and lecturers that meet the global standard. Scholarships should be given to students to study locally instead of overseas. Experts from other nations can be brought in to teach and lecture in local universities instead of having students sent overseas. The funds allocated to send students overseas should be used for the development of local universities instead.

Embassies overseas can also help encourage returnees to move back to their home countries. Lim adds that:

Almost every Asian government facing this brain drain crisis has concocted some form of incentives in terms of tax exemptions, higher salaries, and special privileges, but this strategy bears little fruit. The government of Thailand launched the Reverse Brain Drain Project in 1997. This project aims to create new opportunities for highly skilled Thai migrants to venture into their own research and development projects within their countries as long as it benefits them. The Thai government is providing funds to facilitate these projects in exchange for the information transfer from these migrants. The ultimate aim of this project is to facilitate the return of emigrant Thais and their assimilations back into the work force of Thailand. There have been results since the launch of this project, but it has yet to fully address the brain drain issue—one reason being that only those interested in research and those involved in the field of science will choose to take part in this project. Governments have yet to come up with an effective way to deal with this issue.

Governments should carefully review their immigration policies to open up borders for appropriate talent, writes Antipasado:

The controlled relaxation of stringent immigration policies is something governments should strongly consider as a means of letting young, talented, and skilled professionals contribute to growth in both the countries they are working in and the families back home that they are working for. In Britain for example, there is a so-called Tier 5 Visa (which includes the Youth Mobility Scheme) available to applicants aged 18 to 30 years old. This visa allows them to work in the [country] for a maximum period of 24 months. A similar system would provide needed skilled labor but also provide a vibrant exchange of knowledge and experience within the workforce without the additional burden of integrating the person into the country and providing citizenship guarantees.

Tenzin Dolma, 18, of Tibet, China, suggests opening up Asian universities to foreign students:

Just as our business and economy is globalizing, why not open our door to the varied students who would like to pursue a course in Asian universities. . . . The Western universities believe that they should attract the best and wisest of the brains from all over the globe. This is one thing we should learn from them, that is, making our educational institutions have global exposure. . . . For a Tibetan student like me, many of the choices in the professional courses are closed since I either need to have an Indian citizenship or a big amount of money to enter as a foreign student.

Conclusion

Young Asians see educating and training a skilled workforce as crucial for Asia's continued rise. As Ong, of Singapore, writes:

Education is important not as an end in itself; it is the means through which people gain financial access to a better life through employment, and countries become able to provide this better life through economic growth. It is also the means through which people come to play a more active role in shaping the cultures of their communities and influencing the governance of their countries.

Antipasado, of the Philippines warns that:

Without a skilled workforce to inherit, maintain, and perpetuate the advances made by the previous generation of entrepreneurs, innovators, leaders, and skilled foot soldiers, development will stagnate at best or degenerate at worst. . . . As a young professional myself, I am fortunate to have found a place within a company that has provided me with certain avenues that aren't necessarily available to all people who are my age. I enjoy my work, but there are times when I feel a certain kind of restlessness: the yearning to grow more; an overwhelming anxiety about the future; the constant worrying about the present, and that when all is said and done, we might fall short at the end. I see and talk to a lot of individuals my age who feel the same way. The future does hold a lot of promise, but it is also riddled with plenty of perils. We understand that at the end of the day, we are responsible for our own decisions and the consequences that follow in their wake, but a little help does go a long way.

In order to improve its competitiveness in the future, Asia must prepare its young people for the challenges that lie ahead. " 'Thousands of people are forcing themselves across a narrow footbridge' goes an old Chinese saying, referring to the cutthroat competition that most Asian students have to face in order to study in the crème de la crème of the universities," notes Menon, of India. The widening of this footbridge and the improvement in quality of people crossing it will greatly affect Asia's human capital and ultimately its economic growth.

Essayists Cited

Introduction
Danica Elaine Ang, 22, the Philippines

Education Access
Ashwin Menon, 20, India
Karishma Singh Ahluwalia, 31, India
Avish Acharya, 19, Nepal
Aprakrita Shankar Narayanan, 16, India
Mariyam Thomas, 25, India
Kamanasish Sen, 26, India
Tan Zi Xiang, 16, Singapore
Benjamin Joshua Ong, 20, Singapore
Lưu Ngọc Thảo, 17, Vietnam
Frederick A. Halcon, 31, the Philippines

Education Quality
Kamanasish Sen, 26, India
Ashwin Menon, 20, India
Chandan Kumar, 28, India
Farooq Jamil Alvi, 29, Pakistan
Yassif Nagim, 29, Malaysia
Danica Elaine Ang, 22, the Philippines
Frederick A. Halcon, 31, the Philippines

Future Career
Graeco Paul Antipasado, 25, the Philippines
Jeremy Lim, 18, Malaysia
Avish Acharya, 19, Nepal
Danica Elaine Ang, 22, the Philippines
Tenzin Dolma, 18, China

Conclusion
Benjamin Joshua Ong, 20, Singapore
Graeco Paul Antipasado, 25, the Philippines
Ashwin Menon, 20, India

Chapter 2

Inequality

One man's beard is on fire, another warms his hands on it.
—Kashmiri proverb

Introduction

Deng Xiaoping famously turned his back on the Maoist ideal of equality, adopting economic policies that allowed some people to get rich first. Deng unleashed the raw energy of China's entrepreneurs. Today, the country's 1.1 million millionaires are witness to the success of Deng's vision. China's growth, since reforms began in 1978, has brought more than 600 million people out of poverty.[1] This is an achievement unmatched in human history. At the same time, while China as a whole has become richer and poverty has declined, inequality has increased dramatically. These sorts of growing income disparities, along with persistent poverty, are a source of concern for Tiger Cubs around the region.

East Asia has produced the fastest sustained rate of economic growth in history. First Japan, then the Four Tigers (Hong Kong, Singapore, South Korea, and Taiwan), clocked up record GDP growth, decade after decade of increases in the high single digits or double digits annually. Other countries in the region have also shown impressive performances. Growth in the low single digits would have been regarded as a miracle in the past: England grew only 2 percent a year from 1820 to 1870, the heyday of its nineteenth-century Industrial Revolution.[2] But countries that grow at twice that rate now are regarded as laggards in Asia. China has been outpacing its neighbors, averaging 10.1 percent annual growth since 1978.[3] India's annual growth looks set to remain in the high single digits for decades to come.

From the perspective of the overall economy, this all sounds like good news. Unfortunately, as is true for most countries during periods of rapid economic growth, inequality in much of Asia has widened. Even if everyone in general is better off, there are always losers. Some people actually find their situations worsening. Small farmers are often among those who suffer. Workers who now must compete against imported goods or find their wages or benefits cut as a result of privatization can see their living standards decline in absolute terms. But even for those who are better off, the presence of a newly rich class of the very wealthy can provoke resentment and a political backlash. In Thailand, for example, the urban–rural divide of wealth and power provided much of the fuel for the protracted and violent standoff between protestors and the government in the first half of 2010. In China, the notorious "BMW collision affair" in October 2003 incited a ferocious online assault on China's newly rich population after a wealthy woman abused a farmer for allegedly scratching her car, and then jumped into her car and drove into a crowd of people, killing the farmer's wife.[4] In March 2011, 10,000 young people in Hong Kong protested against a new government budget, claiming it favored the rich. Similar cases of confrontation between rich and poor have occurred across the region. Countries with weak rule of law and poor governance are more prone to these sorts of incidents.

Since 1980, the world has become a more equal place. The Gini coefficient, a widely used and comprehensive measure of income inequality, has declined, indicating more equal income distribution. However, income inequality within a number of Asian countries is on the rise, including China, India, Indonesia, Hong Kong, and Japan.[5] High levels of income disparity leave out a large population of potential consumers. So, in theory, narrowing the gap between the haves and have-nots contributes to social stability and facilitates an economic shift toward domestic consumption. How to do this without discouraging growth is a balancing act that challenges every government.

An increasing amount of attention to the issue has spurred some Asian governments into action. In May 2011, Hong Kong for the first time introduced a minimum wage. China's 12th Five-Year Plan, a set of guidelines for the country's development from 2011 to 2015, seeks to mitigate inequality through increased wages and tax reform. In the Philippines, the government is experimenting with a conditional cash-transfer program to help the poor provide proper medical care and education for their children. Generation Y Asians feel that such efforts are both welcome and needed. In addition, essayists emphasized that sustainable improvement requires governments to find ways to create skilled, well-educated labor forces in order to avoid the trap of overreliance on export-oriented development.

While young Asians are concerned with the ways to raise people up in order to create a more equitable society, they have also called attention to a different group of people: the abject poor. For millions in Asia, the question isn't how to benefit from growth, but merely how to find the next meal. After the signing of the Millennium Development Goals (MDGs) in 2000, an ambitious UN agreement aiming to drastically reduce poverty by 2015, a slew of poverty-reduction programs were implemented in Asian nations. Although China has made the most dramatic reductions in poverty, most countries have made improvements as well.[6] Before the financial crisis hit in 2008, Asia as a whole was on track to achieve the MDGs of halving the numbers of people living on less than $1.00 a day and of people without access to clean water. The 2008–2009 crisis, which stalled progress made toward the anti-poverty targets and slowed development, had pushed 21 million more Asians into extreme poverty by early 2010.[7]

Poverty, along with weak and ineffective governments, means that the poor are by definition vulnerable to everything from natural disasters like typhoons and earthquakes to global economic melt-downs. In spite of improvements, the continent still holds more than half of the world's poor.[8]

Human Development

Young Asians question why wealth gaps should widen at a time of high economic growth. For many Generation Y Asians, the issues underpinning inequality lie in a sense of fairness. Writes Hans Ching, 21, the Philippines:

> For many in Asia, the economic miracle is a deceptive mirage. New business districts are flanked by slums, while cities built from scratch encroach on the land of farmers in which they have toiled for centuries. Many say this is a small price to pay toward progress. But because these situations are so common in the current development of Asian nations, the magnitude of this problem is severe. While Asian countries have seen their economies grow by leaps and bounds through the collective perseverance of their citizens, more marginalized constituents have not been included in this increasingly prosperous society.

Young Asians advocate increasing opportunities for those on the lower end of the spectrum. With suggestions ranging from job cre-ation to education, they look to the market to help balance out Asia.

The images conjured by essayists underline the extent of inequality in some Asian cities. Sarabjit Singh, 26, India, the winner of our essay contest, describes Mumbai, writing:

> There, poverty moves alongside opulence like chocolate in a marble cake. BMWs and Mercedes run over fly-overs that shel-ter shanty towns and slums. And beggars beseech the drivers and the driven when the same cars stop at the next traffic light.

Several young Asians attribute rising tensions to a shift in the mind-set of many have-nots, noting that across Asia, people today feel more entitled to opportunities, and are more aware of those experienced by others. Ching states:

> A revealing psychological implication can be offered by the rise of a meritocratic Asia. Centuries ago, inequality was present, yet it was treated as preordained. One was important no matter which social class he belonged to because people believed that every caste had a purpose in society that complemented each other's functions and existence. Although one may have been impoverished, he also had a sense of self-esteem. Today, due to Western influence and the rise of capitalism, a mindset of meritocracy permeates. Because meritocratic thought dictates that one is in his position as a result of his own actions, society now perceives the poor as lazy and ignorant by not taking the time to study and better themselves, and thus cannot find productive and fulfilling work. . . . There is a certain indignity to feeling left-behind, which ultimately breeds resentment.

Singh expresses similar observations, writing:

> Times have changed—with technology now connecting previously far-flung regions of a country, the underprivileged can now more easily gape at the affluence of their fellow countrymen, potentially inflaming their grievances even further.

This increase in resentment can be seen across Asian countries, where a feeling of what the Chinese call *chou fu*, or hating the rich, pervades. A 2009 survey by the Zhejiang Academy of Social Sciences of more than 1,000 members of the public, including public servants, entrepreneurs, and farmers, found that 96 percent of respondents expressed resentment toward the rich.[9]

Young Asians express concern about violence or social disruption stemming from inequality. Poh Wei Leong, 29, Singapore, cautions:

> In as much as governments are eager to bring the poor to an equal playing field with city dwellers, the poor are also as frustrated that their seemingly feckless governments have forgotten them. Three factors termed as *amplifiers* (natural disasters, internet connectivity, and civil society) have the

potential to magnify the rural poor's angst. The consequence of such is mayhem and near-anarchy at its worst, or another economic upheaval spooking business investors and tourists at its best.

In the same vein, Ching notes:

> With pervasive inequality throughout the region, the nascent resentment from the poor can escalate to social unrest through a catalyst. The mystery about this is that the catalyst can be anything, and can be activated at any time. If a housing bubble bursts in China, it will have [a] serious effect on the millions of migrant workers in factories and construction sites, and ultimately their families back in the countryside. The poor are always the first to be affected in such crises because they have less of a margin to absorb economic losses. This will lead to their expression of frustration against the government and ruling class through force and numbers.

These worries are justified. In several Asian countries, specifically China and India, discontent has led to protests against food costs and high inflation. Tens of thousands of Indian protesters took to the streets in New Delhi in February 2011 against high food prices, which have primarily affected the country's low-income population.[10] Demonstrations in Shanghai turned violent in April 2011 when thousands of truck drivers smashed windows around the port in protest against low wages and increased fuel prices.[11]

Singh is one of several essayists to note that, in addition to a threat of social disruption, social inequality can have negative effects on other aspects of an economy, causing market inefficiencies, unwanted migration, and lack of infrastructure and jobs. He writes:

> In imperfect financial markets—a category even the most open of Asian economies belong to—inequality can trap the poor in an inescapable spiral, shutting them out from access to credit, education, or business opportunities. To add to this, rising inequality increases pressure to redistribute income, adding potentially distorting mechanisms and making the markets even less perfect. In the long run, "a high level of inequality

may actually hinder . . . growth and development prospects" [according to a 2007 report by the Asian Development Bank].

When it comes to closing the gap between the rich and the poor, young Asians are looking for ways to elevate the have-nots. Singh underlines the importance of treating the disease, instead of the symptoms, noting that Asian governments should aim to equalize opportunity. He writes:

Income redistribution or social redress measures as solutions are incomplete, ineffective, or worse because they often follow from a case of mistaken provenance of economic inequality. Numbers that demonstrate a worsening inequality aren't so much a disease that needs a cure, but more a symptom indicative of the real malaise—that unevenly distributed economic growth offers uneven opportunities across peoples, translating into unevenly distributed income and hence economic inequality. In the long run, it is opportunity and not income that we should strive to equalize. It will not eradicate inequality. But it will be an important step towards preventing it from growing further without compromising continued economic growth.

Many young Asians echo this theme of equalizing opportunity, suggesting ways to raise awareness and accountability, as well as to create policy programs that will enable low-income populations to catch up. Ching recommends an international body to monitor development. He writes:

The solution is a concrete shift in priorities. An international commission, the Asian Council for Mutual Prosperity, can be formed to monitor governments' participation in the drive for more inclusive growth. Asian member countries would then sign an agreement that would make them invest in economically empowering the less fortunate in their societies. The commission would also act as a recommending body on how various and different governments should handle this problem, on a country-to-country basis. Rather than being a vague commitment, this agreement would be clear and transparent in how much the government would invest and where.

Singh recommends targeting rural development as a way to increase opportunities, citing the example of Mexico. Between 1999 and 2008, Mexico averaged annual GDP growth of 2.7 percent.[12] During this same period, it also managed to decrease the Gini coefficient from 0.53 to 0.46, the lowest the country had seen for 60 years.[13] Singh writes:

> No doubt, the economies of Latin America and Asia are different, and there are things that worked in Mexico's favor that aren't applicable to Asia. But surely there should be a few ingredients of Mexico's success that can offer Asia a lesson in balancing economic growth with equality of opportunity. There is at least one: the country's focus on rural development. A depreciation in rural poverty contributed significantly to Mexico's economic growth as well as its tempering inequality over the last decade. . . . Between 2000 and 2004, extreme poverty fell almost seven percentage points, which can be explained by development in rural areas, where extreme poverty fell from 42.4 percent to 27.9 percent. . . . According to the World Bank, the factors that contributed to this reduction include "macroeconomic stability . . . and the diversification of income from nonagricultural activities, such as tourism and services"—arguably also applicable in equal measure in at least some parts of emerging Asia.

Similarly, young Asians sought to avoid pushing all citizens into densely populated cities as a means for narrowing the gap between those living in the city and those living in the country. Chandan Kumar, 28, India, writes:

> When it comes to planning urban development, we should look for uniform urban community development rather than creating urban hotspots such as Shanghai and Mumbai, because such a model leads to the polarization of resources. The government tends to allocate more resources to the urban hotspot owing to its whopping requirements arising from the mass migration of workers, ecological imbalance, and pollution, to name a few. In order to support the infrastructure of such hotspot cities, the governments are forced to invest more and more in such cities, thereby creating polarized development of the country on the whole.

Kumar suggests that city planners should utilize a "city-unit" model in order to correct this imbalance and shift governmental resources to a wider range of developing areas, thereby allowing towns to function independently of the resources provided by a city. Kumar writes:

> When I talk about a uniform urban community development, I am not simply referring to the complete urbanization of the society itself. The emphasis is rather on creating multiple independent *city-units*. These city-units will be independent in terms of providing all required resources, such as jobs, food, and advanced education to its population. For example: If a new mineral site is discovered in some tribal area, the government should not look at it as merely a potential mining industry around that region but should also take steps to develop it as an independent city-unit that will leverage its mineral booty to flourish as a whole.

Young Asians look toward education as a means to correct inherent imbalances. Steve Or, 21, Hong Kong, writes that a natural solution "is to enable the social ladder to be climbed more easily. One way to get this done is through education, a major tool for people to learn knowledge and thus enhance productivity." Similarly, Khan Asif Azad, 25, India, notes that providing opportunities is a matter of both situation and education. He encourages education as a way to strengthen equality in Asian nations, writing:

> A classical example like redistributive taxes can be implemented to average out the rich-poor divide in a short time period as already implemented in countries like Japan and Sweden. Higher wage earners can be taxed more as compared to lower wage earners. Also, easier and better access to education will help society gain access to basic amenities of life and transform an individual from being a dependent to a bread winner in a society. Nurturing ideas at college levels, and instilling creative thinking and problem-based learning, will help students prepare better for challenges in life. This also helps children identify their strengths and hence develop them to contribute the most and their best. Political will to take actions, the right to free expression, and freedom to access technology are other measures that impact positively.

Young Asians also look to business in order to reach the bottommost population, arguing that a free-market mechanism will naturally provide more opportunities for young workers looking for better employment. Kensuke Nakahara, 25, Japan, advocates more market opportunities as a means of development, writing:

> Deregulation of economies is good for not only bringing about vitality to the poor person but also . . . overcoming poverty. Now, our world is closer economically than ever; the border between one nation and another is disappearing, and many big companies are trying to make a profit in worldwide businesses. In such a world tide, poor regions have a big point which makes companies' mouths water. They have a reasonable workforce. I think the best way for poor people to overcome poverty is global capitalism. China has made huge economic progress in such a way. In the second quarter of 2010, China overtook Japan in GDP. China has many factories of big foreign companies, and people who work there become richer by receiving salaries from the rich company. The rich company pays a salary for them willingly because their salaries are more reasonable than those of workers in the company's mother country. If poor people have work in good conditions, they will be happy and become richer. I think it is a very good way for poor regions to develop economically, because the advanced knowledge of the global company will become common in the region.

Nakahara notes that encouraging an active market economy will create more investment and job opportunities for those on the lower end of the income scale. He calls upon the government to encourage capitalism:

> Reducing corporate tax is effective for [enticing] global companies. Generally speaking, companies [want] to pay more dividends to their stockholders. They try hard to produce profits in order to repay their investors, who expect growth from the company. It is true that the government's corporate tax income will decrease, but [that] is not bad. If a big company brings wealth to a poor region, other taxes may increase—for

example: consumption tax, income tax, residence tax, liquor or cigarette tax, and so on. [In this] aspect, economic vitality is very important to make a country rich. If poor people can hope to become rich, they may [make] a big effort to achieve it. In such an economy, people can be ambitious. I believe [this] hope in the future can make Asia an economically competitive region. In the future, people who were previously poor may create famous companies.

The recommendations of young Asian thinkers for policy and cultural shifts underline the desire for a more equal Asia, where equal access to opportunities and services will allow more of Asia's citizens to benefit from the region's development.

Poverty Alleviation

Whereas many young Asians look to improve employment opportunities for those on the lower end of the spectrum, others call attention to the 903 million people in Asia (nearly triple the population of the United States) who live on less than $1.25 a day and lack access to adequate food, water, and basic services.[14] For Asia's impoverished populations, the question is not improving life so much as sustaining it.

Young Asians consistently link poverty to a number of other social ills. Zigfred Diaz, 31, the Philippines, writes:

As a result of poverty in Asia, the region has the highest number of malnourished children and one of the poorest healthcare [systems] among the continents. . . . Asia has the highest rate of human trafficking. Asians are lured into false hopes of having good paying jobs in other countries only to find out that they have been trafficked into forced labor. Trafficked women and children are often forced into prostitution and sexual exploitation.

Diaz notes that 1.4 million people in the Asia-Pacific region are in forced-labor situations at any given time, 56 percent of the worldwide total.[15]

What makes things worse is that poverty-stricken families lack upward mobility or the ability to change their situations. Nakahara, of Japan, writes:

> The most crucial problem is the fact that poor people will remain poor in the future. I think a child who is born into a poor family generally has difficulty in receiving advanced education because it takes a huge cost and a poor family cannot pay much money for its child's education. In bad cases, parents regard their children as a [means] to gain income for the family. In the worst case, parents make their child a prostitute. As a result, people who suffer from poverty have little chance to rise from their severe circumstances, and finally poor people begin to give up [trying to] get themselves out of poverty.

Very few essayists look to the government for solutions to poverty, and some, such as Vibhor Bhardwaj, 23, India, worry that government corruption may decrease the effectiveness of poverty-reduction programs. He writes:

> In Asian countries there is no dearth of schemes for the poor, but the management and implementation is always in corrupt and inefficient hands. In India, the National Rural Employment Guarantee Scheme . . . and Sarva Shiksha Abhiyan ("Education for All" Movement) . . . can be put in this category.

In India, these anti-poverty campaigns have come under fire for corrupt practices and misuse of funds. The National Rural Employment Guarantee Scheme, which guarantees 100 days of minimum-wage manual labor to adult members of rural households, faced a social audit after a January 2011 report from the World Bank criticized the program's uneven implementation and alluded to evidence that funds were being misused.[16] Meanwhile, the United Kingdom ordered an inquiry into the Sarva Shiksha Abhiyan scheme in June 2010 after a report from India's Ministry of Human Development called attention to discrepancies in the aid program's audit reports.[17]

Instead of counting solely on the government to alleviate poverty, Generation Y Asians looked to social enterprises as a way to effectively distribute aid to those in need. When discussing the idea of social enterprise, essayists pointed to the theories of the late C.K. Prahalad of the University of Michigan, whose innovative Bottom of the Pyramid theory advocated treating the billions of people who live on less than $2 a day as consumers rather than victims. For young Asians, social enterprises that focus on the poor population provide the most hope for reducing poverty in Asia.

More than one essayist cites Grameen Danone Foods, a social business enterprise started by Group Danone and Grameen Bank of Bangladesh that aims to provide Bangladeshi children with key nutrients otherwise missing from their diets. The company gauges success based on the number of jobs created in rural Bangladesh, the tangible improvements to children's health within regions of distribution, and the positive environmental effects, rather than on profits, which are put back into the venture.[18] Joseph James, 29, India, praises the program as "a testimony that initiatives of this kind are truly feasible and scalable."

Conclusion

Widening inequality is seen as a negative consequence of the rapid growth experienced by the continent in the past few decades. Wealth has been amassed, yet the perception among young Asians is that only a small proportion of people are benefiting. As Asia's economic pie continues to grow, populations are demanding a greater slice of this pie, or the opportunity to work hard so they can gain a share. Asia's poor are often seen as a burden, but they can also be a resource if the systemic barriers that have trapped them in poverty can be lowered. Only then will many Asians be able to exercise their entrepreneurial spirit and willingness to work hard in order to build a better future for themselves and their families.

Essayists Cited

Human Development
Hans Nathan L. Ching, 21, the Philippines
Sarabjit Singh, 26, India
Poh Wei Leong, 29, Singapore

Chandan Kumar, 28, India
Steve Or, 21, Hong Kong
Khan Asif Azad, 25, India
Kensuke Nakahara, 25, Japan

Poverty Alleviation
Zigfred Diaz, 31, the Philippines
Kensuke Nakahara, 25, Japan
Vibhor Bhardwaj, 23, India
Joseph James, 29, India

Chapter 3

Demographics

At 70 you are but a child; at 80 you are merely a youth; and at 90 if the ancestors invite you into heaven, ask them to wait until you are 100 and then you might consider it.

—Japanese proverb

Introduction

Asia faces two extreme demographic futures. On the one hand, developing countries like India, Indonesia, and Pakistan have large and growing populations, putting a heavy burden on sustained economic growth. On the other hand, developed economies including Japan, Singapore, Taiwan, South Korea, and Hong Kong are facing the challenge of an unbalanced age structure as older populations swell at a time of low birthrates. Strikingly, China, the largest country in the world, is facing three problems—continued population growth, rapid aging, and low birthrates.

China and India are already the two most populous countries in the world; Indonesia and Pakistan are also high on the list of the world's largest nations. Together, these four countries comprise about 3 billion people, or 43 percent of the world's population.[1] Asia will remain the largest contributor to global population growth, at least in the next four decades. Population growth means growing demand for basic education, healthcare, food, and shelter, as well as for employment. A big concern of the Tiger Cubs is that governments do not have the capacity to provide for these basic needs. The problem of overpopulation, where population outgrows available resources, may lead to a lower quality of life and a host of economic and social problems for Asian countries.

Conversely, developed Asia is currently experiencing rapid population aging. Japan's population aged 60 or over will account for 34 percent of the country's total population by 2020 and 40 percent by 2035. In 2010, there were only 1.8 working-age persons (between 15 and 59) for each Japanese aged 60 or over. The forecast for 2020 is 0.65 working persons per elderly Japanese.[2] This change will impose pressures on society, as smaller workforces support larger retired populations, as well as on individuals supporting their retired parents.

The consequences for this go far beyond economics. An aging Asia may mean a more risk-averse, slower-moving Asia. It will bring issues of generational equity to the fore. The Tiger Cub generation worries that an aging Asia may upend the region's traditional deference to elders. As Megawati Wijaya, 30, Indonesia, points out:

> In the 1990s and 2000s, Asia may have been the youthful continent—full of dreams and possibilities. But in 2020, Asia may very well be the ultimate aging continent—slow in political reforms, frail in terms of innovation and productivity, and rather pale in economic outlook—no thanks to the large size of its aging population. Young Asians concerned about their parents' aging ask themselves, "How many more years can my parents work and stay healthy?" and more crucially, "Will my savings be enough to provide for their healthcare as they

grow old?" They could be no longer concerned with nosy parents' prodding questions of "Why are you not married yet?" or "When will you give us grandchildren?"

Wijaya recounts a story about her friend's grandmother, who had been hospitalized for more than a month after a hard fall in the bathroom. The friend is concerned about her parents' savings drying up after paying for the home stay. The friend is also worried that "by the time my grandmother dies, it will be my parents' turn to be looked after, and I will be the next [cash cow]."

A related concern is the soaring demand for healthcare services and the costs of healthcare infrastructure and medicine. A growing proportion of retired citizens will strain government healthcare systems. Many developing countries in Asia already have limited resources and financing for healthcare. China, India, and Indonesia spend less than 10 percent of their governments' budgets on healthcare, compared to almost 20 percent for Japan and the United States, and have less than one-fifth of the physicians, nurses, and hospital beds per capita.

These two very different demographic trends each pose challenges for Asia's economic and social development. Countries must confront them head-on in order to avoid what in a worst-case scenario could be a difficult demographic destiny.

Population Growth

Overpopulation is a problem for many countries in Asia, particularly India, Pakistan, Indonesia, and China. Up until 2050, India and Pakistan will be the two largest contributors to global population growth, according to the UN. Asia is projected to be home to about 400 million more people, adding to the current 4.2 billion.[3] However, the region will struggle to find the resources—both natural and human— to support these growing populations. If, indeed, food and other natural resources are embarking on long-term price increases, poor countries will suffer the most.

Young Asians are especially concerned about the inability of governments to provide basic services and jobs for these large populations, and about the emergence of other social and economic problems. Stevenson Q. Yu, 29, the Philippines, writes:

What happens to poor countries with burgeoning populations? In these countries, governments struggle to provide even basic services to citizens. The lower spending power of the populace makes the country a less-attractive market, limiting the number of jobs available. The sheer number of people in the labor force means that competition for jobs will be very fierce. Invariably, this leads to widespread unemployment and poverty—and criminality.

Danica Elaine Ang, 22, the Philippines, acknowledges the relationship between overpopulation and population control policy (although she also argues that looking at population growth simply as a problem is wrong):

More often than not, overpopulation is seen as a hindrance to the pursuit of economic prosperity given the lack of capacity of Asian national governments, the majority of which are developing countries, to sustain the growing number of mouths to feed and bodies to provide services for. This then results in a growing clamor for legislation and implementation of population control policies.

The lack of basic services and jobs to go around may even lead to territorial disputes. Lưu Ngọc Thảo, 17, Vietnam, who comes from a country that has had disputes with China and Cambodia over territorial borders, says:

Another acute problem is that when there are more people, there [is] more demand for food, clothing, equipment, houses, and energy. As a consequence, countries tend to get involved in fights for natural resources as well as in disputes over land and territory. These disagreements, therefore, break down the peace of the whole region and may lead to war.

As more and more young people migrate to urban areas looking for better opportunities, Asian cities have experienced astounding growth, with populations doubling in the past 35 years. More than half of the world's urban populations already live in Asian cities.[4] China will add at least 100 cities with more than half a million residents to its current 236 cities of this size by 2025.[5] In India, the number of slum dwellers is approaching 100 million.[6] Vineet Kumar, 21, India, predicts:

> Over-urbanization due to unplanned and hurried growth of cities and metropolises (which is true of most of the Asian countries) is going to increase in the next decade and has been a major factor in lack of appropriate sanitary conditions, over-crowding, inhuman living conditions, poor health facilities, and lack of basic necessary amenities of life. Problems of slums can be attributed in a broader way to increasing populations.

Many in the current young generation of Asians have grown up at a time of various population-control policies, from less-restrictive government measures (such as improved prenatal healthcare, promotion of family planning, and subsidies for families with fewer children) in South Korea, Taiwan, Thailand, and Indonesia to China's stricter one-child policy, which was introduced in 1978. By one estimate, China's controversial measure has prevented 400 million births in the country.[7] China has experienced a striking decline in fertility from very high (5.9 in 1965) to very low (1.8 in 2009).[8] Economic development almost invariably leads to lower fertility rates, but China's drop is so dramatic that much of it can be attributed to the one-child policy. Whereas China's one-child policy has been criticized by the international community on social, moral, and economic grounds, the generation that has grown up under such policies has mixed feelings about the effectiveness of such initiatives.

Overpopulation appears to be such a serious challenge for Asian countries that young people from countries lacking restrictive policies feel that more controversial and extreme measures may need to be taken. Indeed, young essayists from South Asia support more stringent policies. Saurov Ghosh, 29, India, argues that "governments need to understand that a fundamental right cannot be called a right if it's equally responsible for subjugating and marginalizing the right to education, health, safety and respectability, and the development of society." Ghosh suggests that "birth control, one-child policies, incentives for family planning, and people's support for population control . . . is the way forward" for Asian governments.

However, these same young Asians who support population control policies broadly disagreed with China's one-child policy, calling it "repressive," as well as highlighting consequences of the initiative. Although the policy has been effective in curbing the country's rampant population growth, some young Asians worry that checking population forcefully may create social problems like a worsening gender ratio and a shortage of young workers. Warns Yu:

> China's one-child policy has been very effective in curbing population. Such a drastic approach is not without consequence, however. China's population is rapidly aging, *and* it faces a unique gender imbalance that could leave 24 million eligible bachelors without wives by 2020.

China's blunt one-child policy represents one extreme when it comes to population control. At the other extreme are calls for more education, especially moral education. Lu·u stresses the importance of promoting social harmony:

> The key to open the door of a shining future for Asia is education, or the upgrading of social knowledge levels, with standards of social morality. More and more, Asia is rediscovering the true values of its traditional religions, such as Confucianism, Taoism, and Buddhism, which play an important role in stabilizing the society. . . . The authorities and governments should educate people on population and sex at an appropriate age, to help them understand that social and economic problems are two closely related issues: that they form a virtuous circle in which each factor is built upon another, lending strength to develop the other further.

Vineet Kumar also suggests educating people about the benefits of family planning, particularly through media:

> More than providing family planning tools and equipment, it is important to provide mass education about the ill effects of [large] populations. State-owned mass media (radio, TV, etc.) and the press should be utilized in the most efficient way to create a general consciousness regarding population. The broad

objective of any such programs would be to influence the rate and pattern of population growth in socially desirable directions.

Specifically, he also suggests tying the call to slow population growth to religious and cultural values:

Religious attitudes, cultural norms and values, and ethnic beliefs are the most important reasons for the increased population growth of Islamic countries in Asia, but a patient and carefully carved approach by taking the government and religious leaders into confidence can be initiated, and general awareness among the public creating mass movements can be implemented.

Vineet Kumar further notes that Asian leaders should highlight overpopulation as a bigger problem in global forums:

One of the failures that is often alluded to about Asian countries is their inability to recognize the importance and significance of this problem, which is reflected in their priorities in the world forums and international summits where there is very little discussion of population explosions, and where terrorism, climate change, global warming, health problems, ecological imbalance, [and so on], are given more importance. . . . Hence a shift in focus more toward population and its troubles, and an understanding of its gravity, should be given importance.

Young Asians offer various other solutions for the overpopulation challenge. They point out that governments should invest in human capital to make their rising populations into assets for future development. Ang says:

Instead of looking at this projection as a problem that worsens the resources deficit, the rising population in Asia should be seen as an asset, a potential which ought to be tapped and maximized. For Asian countries to keep up with the demands of globalization and reap the benefits of its expected rising population, particular emphasis and attention must be given to human capital development that is deemed to result in economic development, that is, investment in human capital must be given considerable priority.

Investing in human capital via education has the added benefit of lowering fertility rates. Vineet Kumar also mentions:

Education seems the best way to reduce population and is a wonderful contraceptive. Awareness among masses regarding the unending evil of population growth should be given importance. The most important way to achieve it is by strong political will and effective policy measures. War-level preparation is needed to keep the population under control since sustainable development and growth can be realized in practice only when the product of economic activities matches with the number of consumers.

Overpopulation in cities can be minimized by narrowing the gap between urban standards of living and those in rural areas. This is a policy focus of the Chinese government's 12th Five-Year Plan, which runs from 2011 to 2015, which aims to institute a comprehensive safety net covering healthcare and pensions for farmers, improvements in water and electricity infrastructure in rural areas, and agriculture tax reform. In South Korea, government policies designed to slow the flow of people from rural to urban areas have been in place since the early 1970s.[9] However, the country's lack of success in this regard reflects the difficulty in implementing such policies. In India, efforts have been made to improve the living standard of rural residents in all its five-year plans; measures have included provision of social services like health and education as well as assistance to individual families living below the poverty line.[10] However, Piyush Kumar, 25, India, thinks that government policies are focused too much on big cities, and that governments should focus more on towns and small cities. He suggests:

The only possible solution to prevent people from fleeing to cities is by reducing the difference in opportunities between the two areas. . . . There should be special incentives to set up large offices in small towns and cities. This is not going to be easy because smaller towns lack the most basic infrastructure and amenities. But that is the only way forward to keep the success story of Asia going on. The current setup of concentrating development in big cities needs to be changed. There should be corporate offices in small cities which should be very well connected by road, rails, and other means of transport. This benefits all the involved parties.

He also thinks that higher taxes for city dwellers would take away many of the economic benefits of living in a city and help neutralize migration:

> The government can fix the price of fuels (petrol, diesel, etc.) according to the size of the city. There should be a separate tax called city tax levied on products and services. This tax should vary from city to city, highest for the largest metro areas and zero for villages. This will make fuel cheaper for farmers as well as corporations which locate outside the city. This can also make electricity available to corporations as well as the common man at a reduced rate on the basis of the population of the city. A less-populated city should be taxed less, and there should be reduced tax on property and reduced income tax. This will bring a level of equality in the form of equal savings of people in similar jobs across cities or metro areas and compensate for the variance in payouts according to cities.

Aging

Over the next decade, several major Asian economies, including China, Japan, and South Korea, will all have rapidly aging populations. This demographic trend will pose great challenges for governments in terms of the provision of social services and age-friendly infrastructure. The population aged 60 or over in all of Asia is estimated to grow to 594 million in 2020, from 414 million in 2010.[11]

Although social safety nets are being built as Asian nations become richer, even in wealthy countries young Asians do not expect to rely solely on the government to provide care for their aging parents.

Indeed, for many Asians of the Tiger Cub generation, finding good care for aged parents is becoming similar to the sort of struggle to secure school and university entrance places that defined their childhoods. Wijaya, of Indonesia, writes:

> In China, the impact of the one-child policy, first enforced for newborns in 1979, [is] expected to take [its] full toll within the next decade. In 2020, China's first batch of little emperors and empresses will be in their 40s. Their parents will be in their 60s and 70s—too old for work—and will have to depend solely on their one and only [child] for care. . . . Not unlike an entry to the Ivy League universities, a quick, successful admission to a good elderly home in Singapore is a much-coveted prize, with tips and success stories circulated among people who want to know how to repeat the feat. Many Chinese still live by meager wages, and having no sibling to share the burden, taking care of old parents may prove to be costly and strenuous for the young amid the rising costs of living.

Countries with growing numbers of the aged may become inhospitable for business, no matter how friendly their tax or business attraction policies. Japan is the most extreme example of this phenomenon. The population is starting a long decline. Companies struggle to grow in a deflationary environment characterized by an aging and shrinking nation. As a result, Japanese multinationals are forced to look abroad for growth. That leads to the possibility of an economic hollowing-out that feeds on itself. Wijaya argues:

> Most companies set to expand globally will ditch countries with aging populations, choosing to set roots instead in countries with an abundant young labor force that will be cheaper, easier to train, and more productive. Homegrown businesses in countries with dominant aging populations may need to expand overseas to capture bigger markets or to be nearer to customers with strong spending power. As they move their businesses overseas, gone with them will be the potential job opportunities at home. Talents will flow freely to where the jobs are, and this may cause brain drain in the countries with

aging populations as their homegrown talents flee home for greener pastures abroad.

In addition, Wijaya notices that there is limited international experience in tackling aging issues, including the lack of facilities for the aged, healthcare, and pension schemes. As a result, Asians have to learn by doing:

> For many countries, coping with aging populations will be largely trial-and-error exercises in public policy—they will create policies as they go along when they realize a new problem brewing. One's stance on aging populations will be an important political issue that can make or break a politician, and I would imagine every public policy school in Asia will rush to open a new branch of study dedicated to aging population issues in years to come.

Aging populations also put stress on countries' healthcare systems. Gemlyn George, 26, India, runner-up of our essay contest, points out:

> The two big engines of economic growth in Asia (South Asia and China) have healthcare systems that are fragmented, suffer huge deficits of manpower and facilities, and are potential flashpoints of anger for young populations that are increasingly demanding the best possible care. Further complicating the scenario is the presence of traditional systems of medicine, which often operate in unregulated areas without proper checks and controls.

Young Asians point out that Asia must cope with this aging population on three levels: government, business, and individual. First of all, Asia needs a strong social security system. Wijaya says:

> Here comes the need for governments to put in place a more stable and reliable social security system. Social security has to meet three characteristics: It has to be sufficient to meet the rising healthcare costs; it has to be foolproof to abuse; and it has to preserve the dignity of the elderly.

She cites U.S. President Franklin Roosevelt's vision of social security in 1935 as a model beyond its time, because it advocated the financing of Social Security from payroll taxes rather than from general government revenues. Similarly, Singapore's compulsory Central Provident Fund (CPF) savings, in which employer and employee contribute a certain percentage of salaries into retirement savings, helps citizens prepare for old age.

Governments can also design cities to better accommodate the needs of the aged. "Besides a reliable social security system, governments have to arrange for special living space for an aging population," Wijaya writes. She cites research by the World Health Organization (WHO) of 33 global cities that found a need for elderly-friendly access to public transport, outdoor spaces, and buildings, as well as for appropriate housing, community support, and health services. The WHO launched the Global Network of Age-Friendly Cities in 2010 to help cities to create such spaces.

Healthcare also needs to become more affordable for retirees. One solution is to use information technologies and also employ retired doctors to lower costs while ensuring quality services for patients, suggests Ravleen Kaur, 16, India:

> More than 50 percent of patients can actually be managed safely through tele-consultation. Who should man these centers? Ideally we can get the recently retired doctors from the national health services. At 65, they still have 10 years of productivity that can be well-utilized. A well-functioning tele-medicine hub at a regional and national level can significantly reduce the workload on local outpatients and governmental hospitals.

To relieve the strain of rising healthcare demands on government budgets, Asian countries could look to public-private partnerships to finance healthcare. Some countries have been successful, George writes:

> The Middle Eastern countries employ a mix of public (funded by petrodollars, heavily subsidized) and private sector hospitals (paid for by insurance or direct fees) to take care of their health systems. Other nations like Singapore and South Korea mandate universal insurance coverage for everyone, paid for to varying degrees by the individual, the employer, and the rest subsidized by the government (40 to 60 percent depending on

the country). The government also has healthcare safety nets for those who cannot afford insurance.

Likewise, Siddharth Surendra Gadre, 22, India, supports a public-private model to ensure healthcare services for a broader group of patients:

The governments need to interfere. Thus, in partnership with private players, they should try to cut the chain between the origin of service and the people who are actually using the service. Costs of the profit margins of the intermediaries therefore can be saved. Governments should supply cheap capital to hospitals and to pharmacy companies and thus help them to lower costs (which will automatically drop significantly due to cheap capital). Also, policies must be forced upon hospitals setting fixed, low-yet-sufficient profit levels. So to earn large profits, large volumes will be needed, forcing hospitals to extend their services to every individual.

Besides partnering with governments, the business community can also contribute in other ways. Wijaya adds:

Not all is gloom in countries with aging populations. Sharp-minded entrepreneurs will discover that growing aging populations mean a new consumer market. In many countries, silver industries—targeting the special needs of aging populations—have been growing. Their businesses range from providing services, such as training nurses, to high-tech industries such as designing robots to help the elderly in their daily activities. The business potential is limitless—there could be guided tours specially designed for the elderly or catering services that provide nutritious diets for this group. As 2020 approaches, states should encourage more entrepreneurs to enter into the sector by providing incentives such as tax rebates.

On the individual level, Wijaya encourages a change in stereotypes and mindsets regarding elderly populations:

On the individual level, negative stereotypes and mindsets regarding the aging population have to be changed. Needless to say this is the most difficult task of all. Instead of building hardware facilities, stakeholders have to alter the perception widely believed that the elderly are noncontributing members of society. Many countries have pushed back retirement ages to allow the elderly to remain at work. They may be demoted or asked to perform simpler tasks. Still, this is a welcome approach to boost the confidence of the elderly themselves and to convince society that the elderly are not practically useless. . . . Governments and companies should continue promoting age-friendly policies at workplaces. Working beyond retirement age, however, has to be a choice, not a must. The elderly should work because they want to, not because they have no choice due to the absence of old age savings or reliable social security. Policy makers must not treat the issue with cold hearts and a set of rigid rules. Flexibility is of utmost importance to ensure that the unique needs of different elderly populations can be met.

Conclusion

Asian countries must address extremes in terms of population and age structure. Most countries are encountering one of two problems—high birthrates and the threat of overpopulation or low birthrates and an aging population. Overpopulation threatens jobs and quality of life, and may lead to other social issues. A rapidly aging Asia means increasing demand for healthcare and other social services but a relatively smaller working population to support the needs of elders.

Resolving these demographic challenges requires a change in ingrained cultures and values. Whereas this is difficult in the short term, many young Asians believe that effective government interventions could play a significant role in educating and changing family and individual attitudes and behaviors toward sex selection and family size. Young Asians also suggest that resolving demographic problems will improve social harmony. Stressing this value will help people see the benefits of family planning and respect for the elderly.

In the more immediate term, young Asians point out that governments can partner with the business community to provide better healthcare services for populations, especially for the aged, primarily by using information technology and building better healthcare infrastructure to reduce dependency burdens.

Essayists Cited

Introduction
Megawati Wijaya, 30, Indonesia

Population Growth
Stevenson Q. Yu, 29, the Philippines
Danica Elaine Ang, 22, the Philippines
Lưu Ngọc Thảo, 17, Vietnam
Vineet Kumar, 21, India
Saurov Ghosh, 29, India
Piyush Kumar, 25, India

Aging
Megawati Wijaya, 30, Indonesia
Gemlyn George, 26, India
Ravleen Kaur, 16, India
Siddharth Surendra Gadre, 22, India

Part II

ASIA'S COMMUNITY

Chapter 4

Environment

If we do not change our direction, we are likely to end up where we are headed.

—Chinese proverb

Introduction

Asia's economic and population growth have taken a brutal toll on the region's environment. Environmental issues regularly rank among the top worries for Asians overall, with environment-related issues often of higher concern than among people in other parts of the world.[1] There is plenty to worry about. Several essayists note that the World Bank says 16 of the world's 20 most-polluted cities are in China. Others pointed to World Health Organization (WHO) data estimating that Asia accounts for two-thirds of the 800,000 premature deaths caused globally by air pollution.

Indeed, if judged by the number of entries, energy and environmental issues are the most pressing challenges facing Asia—more than any other subject. Many of these submissions read as though they are dispatches sent from the front lines of a climate war.

There is no doubt that Asia is on the front lines of climate change. Hundreds of millions of Asians live near oceans or rivers. Rising sea levels and ever-more-frequent flooding and other natural disasters mean that more people—especially the poor—are likely to be hurt by the impact of climate change. Bangladesh Prime Minister Sheikh Hasina called her country "the most vulnerable nation in the world." At the 2009 Copenhagen conference on climate change she stated, "The refugees caused by climate change increase day by day. The rising sea levels and rising temperatures are destroying the habitat of fish and the lives of our fishermen." Increasing "natural disasters, erosion of river banks, and salinization of rivers" endanger the lives of "millions of households engaged in agriculture."[2]

The Tiger Cub generation shows an increasing concern with the environment. To take a dramatic incident mentioned by one essayist: One Singaporean groom marrying a diving enthusiast put a picture of a dead shark on each seat at his wedding banquet rather than serve shark fin soup, long considered a must-have delicacy at Chinese weddings.[3] Youth have been involved in driving a number of environmental campaigns in a region where environmental awareness is on the rise, from fighting shark slaughter to working for energy efficiency, as China's Youth Climate Action Network does with its 52 university affiliates. The group, founded in 2007, has targeted a 20 percent reduction in greenhouse gas emissions at these universities by 2012.[4] In the western Chinese city of Lanzhou, Zhao Zhong founded Green Camel Bell, a civic environmental organization, when he was in his early twenties.[5] Research, not surprisingly, shows that "many youth are increasingly concerned about the environment and with finding sustainable ways of living in harmony with each other, and with the Earth," according to *Young People and the Environment: An Asia-Pacific Perspective*.[6]

Essayists are divided between blaming the West and accepting that their countries need to take urgent measures on their own. Sibtain Naqvi, 28, Pakistan, says:

Talk to the government and one only hears of the mega-projects and GDP figures. Most are even unwilling to acknowledge the issue of climate change. "If we start protecting every tree and forest we would still be living in the jungle," is the baffling response of a minister in the Pakistan government. On being told of climate change and its impending effects on the weather, he shrugged them off as "hippie theories."

Water issues are an especially pressing concern. Water, it is often said, will become the new oil—increasingly scarce and correspondingly expensive. A number of young Asian writers have pointed out the problems, ranging from disease to war, that a shortage of clean water could bring. The bigger problem for many Asians is less absolute scarcity than the problem of filthy water—water contaminated by chemicals, disease, or animal or human waste. As weather becomes more erratic, ever-larger groups of people are buffeted between too much water and not enough. Many of these problems can be solved with better governance, better technology, and more rational economics. But there's little doubt that even with the best of policies, Asia's 4.2 billion people will put extraordinary pressure on water supplies.

Essayists raise other environmental issues, from marine waste and pollution to green branding to forestry. Tidal, solar, wind, micro-hydro power generation, and nuclear power are all mentioned as part of Asia's energy solutions. Some ideas are far-reaching, even fanciful. One young Asian, for example, writes of the possibilities of piezo-electricity, the process where human activities, from walking through a turnstile to running on an exercise treadmill, are used to generate electricity.

Food and agriculture are closely tied with environmental problems. Many young writers are concerned about Asia's looming food crisis. Recommendations range from better national land use plans to more credit to help individual farmers. One essayist wants more outsourcing of food production from rich countries to poor ones. Other solutions included more regional cooperation, perhaps even a regional food bank. Many writers point to the pressing issue of hunger, citing UN figures that 578 million Asians are undernourished.[7]

Energy is a related issue. Worries range from peak oil—will our fossil fuel reserves inevitably start declining?—to the potential for social unrest that rising costs and lack of access to affordable energy will cause. The lack of energy infrastructure is one worry; another is that although aspirations for a more energy-intensive lifestyle are high, there is a recognition that not everyone can live like Americans. Solutions include more research and development leading to new technologies, public education, government policies favoring green initiatives, and more regional and international collaboration.

Natural Disasters

Asia has more natural disasters than any other region in the world. Wikipedia cites sources noting that nine of the world's 10 deadliest natural disasters have been in Asia. Eeman Siddiqui-Malik, 27, Pakistan, cites British consultancy Maplecroft as saying that Bangladesh, Indonesia, Iran, and Pakistan are among the countries most vulnerable to natural disasters. Part of that susceptibility reflects the region's vast size, but much of it reflects Asia's large and dense population. The 4.2 billion people living in Asia represent about 60 percent of the global population, yet live on just 30 percent of its land area. Many live in coastal regions or along rivers. Typhoons, earthquakes, and, of course, the deadly 2004 and 2011 tsunamis have taken hundreds of thousands of lives in the past decade. The 2004 Indian Ocean tsunami alone killed 230,000 people, while Cyclone Nargis in 2008 resulted in an estimated 146,000 deaths in Myanmar.

Pakistan experienced some of the most severe floods in its history in the summer of 2010. Thousands were killed, and 20 million were displaced from their homes, writes Naqvi, of Pakistan, as she describes the reality of what the disaster meant to one villager as well as to the nation:

> Sultan Ahmed gazes at his drowned village. "Years of toil and most of my possessions lie under that water," he remarks ruefully. "My life here is finished and we will have to move to the city." Sultan is a victim of floods that have swept down from the foothills of the Himalayas in Pakistan and across the country. Most of the people in this once-lush land don't even understand the reason for this calamity. While climate change is debated in Copenhagen, for people like Sultan it is a harsh reality, albeit a mysterious one. . . . The number of people displaced is larger than the populations of 132 countries recognized by the UN. Imagine the entire population of

Sri Lanka or Chile being rendered homeless and you will get an idea of the catastrophe. One-fifth of the country is under water and the damage to crops alone has been estimated to be $2.8 billion, with billions more in infrastructure damage. The aid pledged so far is nearing $1 billion. This money could have gone for green solutions, poverty alleviation, renewable energy, and a host of things much needed in the region were it not for the climatic changes being brought about by the environmental damage.

Siddiqui-Malik notes the disproportionate impact that natural disasters have on the poor. The poor have little to lose, yet they often lose everything. Those at the bottom of the pyramid typically don't have insurance, government grants, or loans to help them get started again. "The severity inflicted by such hazards is directly related to the poverty levels of a country and its community," she writes. Poor places are most vulnerable to begin with—houses are often built in marginal areas, vulnerable to flooding, or poorly constructed and susceptible to earthquakes. Siddiqui-Malik continues:

> Poor communities do not have the capacity to address the risks imposed by the catastrophes, and once struck they don't recover from the loss, getting buried deeper in poverty; hence they are caught in a vicious circle. There is a significant difference in the adaptive capabilities of a developed vis-à-vis a developing nation towards building infrastructure, due to scarce resources and the financial implications. They are already burdened with a large population, poor technology, and education costs, and they often promote economic development at the cost of damaging their eco-environment. Therefore, national and regional efforts for natural disaster reduction should be closely linked with poverty alleviation and economic- and social-development activities.

Siddiqui-Malik counsels a wide-ranging philosophy of "preparedness, prevention, and mitigation." Looking in detail at the history of natural-disaster mitigation in Asia, she contends:

> With effective measures in place, Asia can successfully relieve the impact of disasters. To achieve this, regional cooperation

and exchange should be strengthened. Some of the region's countries, notably Japan, have much to teach others, from monitoring and early warning signals of disasters, to risk evaluations, disaster forecasts, and rapid reaction.

Progress has been made since the founding of the Asian Disaster Reduction Center in 1998. Based in Kobe, Japan, the Center works both to help communities prepare for disaster and to respond when calamities occur. Siddiqui-Malik writes:

Most Asian governments have upgraded their civil defense capabilities for the rescue of people from endangered areas, through the mobilization of armed forces or the organization of volunteers in the local communities, in response to threats of disaster. Many countries have appointed a national committee or a central organization to coordinate. Although their effectiveness can raise many eyebrows, at least and more importantly, almost all countries have accepted in principle the need to integrate disaster prevention and environmental protection strategies into their national development plans.

While a number of regional initiatives have been put in place, particularly following the 2004 Indian Ocean tsunami, Siddiqui-Malik would like to see a more extensive effort:

I visualize the formation of a council comprising disaster management experts, geologists, economists, scientists, philanthropists, engineers, and project managers from all over the region. These experts would be responsible for analyzing each country with respect to the type of natural hazard threats that it is susceptible to, study the present capabilities, and gauge how effective they are. These experts would not only provide recommendations but share standardized tools and techniques of loss estimation, damage assessment, disaster record maintenance, and distribution of relief.

Siddiqui-Malik's vision for the organization is that it would have teeth—including the power to impose fines for noncompliance. It would also have a significant role in promulgating best practices to specialists, whether they are architects and engineers, urban planners, or agricultural experts, and in promoting public education. Perhaps its most important role would be in enabling a rapid response in the case of a crisis. One grim-but-necessary task is to ensure best practices are followed with the discovery, identification, and burial of bodies. It would also conduct research into how climate change affects humans. Siddiqui-Malik says that governments can also play a role by promoting farming practices that enable farmers to weather climatic variations, for example, by using drought-resistant crop varieties, and helping farmers increase their ability to adapt to long-term change. She writes:

> To some extent, countries can prepare themselves for natural disasters by adapting to their physical environment. Possible measures include land-use planning to avoid construction on seismic fault lines, in vulnerable coastal regions, and on river shorelines; adoption of standards aimed at ensuring that buildings are resistant to shocks like earthquakes and hurricanes; mitigation of environmental degradation like soil erosion that can increase the impact of disasters; and engineering interventions, such as the creation of dams for flood control, dikes to reroute flood waters, and seawalls to break storm surges.

The litany of natural disasters continues. The devastating March 11, 2011, earthquake and tsunami that ravaged the northeastern coast of the main Japanese island of Honshu and led to one of the world's most serious nuclear accidents is a reminder that even the wealthiest countries are not immune from natural disasters. Siddiqui-Malik suggests:

> The goal for Asia 2020 should be to turn disasters into benefits. As consequences, these disasters also bring with them benefits, which if mobilized properly can be truly a boon for the Asian community. Energy from the water of floods and winds of storms can be utilized into making electricity which already is a scarce resource in nations such as mine. Lava from volcanic eruptions is useful construction material. Floods leave behind river deltas which prove to be the most fertile agricultural lands. In the future, mankind must strive to find ways of controlling the impact of natural disasters and transforming their consequences into useful natural resources.

Water

Too much water. Not enough water. The extremes of flood and drought are all too common throughout Asia. Glaciers are melting, sea levels are rising. Even when there is enough water, all too often there is not enough clean water. These are global problems, but nowhere do they affect more people than in Asia. Soyen Park, 25, South Korea, cites figures noting that agriculture accounts for 84 percent of Asia's water use, but it is riddled with inefficiencies. About half the region's water is wasted.

Young Asians point out the importance of water for economic development and worry about coming water conflicts in Asia. There are calls for collaboration rather than competition. Hydro storage in Nepal could mitigate floods in Bangladesh. Bhutanese hydropower could be sold to electricity-short neighbors. But cross-border collaboration is likely to be slow, and much of it is, in the end, a zero-sum game of wrangling over water rights. That means countries must do all they can to maximize the efficiency with which they use their water resources. The alternative is grim, as several essayists detail in writing about their countries' water shortages.

Shreyans Jain, 20, India, describes the arrival of a water tanker in the upper-class South Delhi neighborhood of Vasant Kunj during the water-scarce summer of 2009:

By the time I could reach the water tanker, hundreds of other colony members had already lined up with buckets and pots and mugs in hands. It was impossible to give water to everyone, and soon some people started bribing the official. This did not go down well with others who called it unethical, and soon a fight picked up. In the heat of the moment, a few words were exchanged, and the situation suddenly got violent. Luckily, some sane people intervened and the fight stopped. As I went back to my flat empty-handed, I could not help but wonder that if this was the situation in a supposedly rich area of India's most pampered city, what would be the state of India's villages?

Park describes a similar situation in South Korea:

> When I arrived in Gangwon-do, I was greeted by empty
> water bottles rolling around the front yard instead of a big
> welcoming smile. It turned out that the province had been
> tortured by the worst drought in 23 years. During two days,
> the only available water source was from the plastic contain-
> ers that my friend's grandma was lucky enough to fill when
> the water truck came by. Other elderly citizens who live by
> the hillsides had to come down with water bottles. Suddenly,
> washing one's face or brushing one's teeth became a privi-
> lege given only to people in the city, and doing laundry was
> unthinkable.

Unsurprisingly, there are worries about water wars. Jain writes:

> There's a serious potential for conflict between countries,
> with disputes stemming from the Euphrates and Tigris
> Rivers among Turkey, Syria, and Iraq; the Jordan River
> between Israel, Lebanon, Jordan, and the Palestine terri-
> tories; the Mekong River between China, Myanmar, Laos,
> Cambodia, Thailand, and Vietnam; the Indus Basin between
> China, Pakistan, and India; and the scarce water resources
> between Kazakhstan, Kyrgyzstan, Tajikistan, Turkmenistan,
> and Uzbekistan.

Solutions to Asia's water crisis range from the technological—
better water treatment, water harvesting, and greater efficiency of
use—to the political and economic. As with many other issues, access
to water must include good governance. Corrupt governments don't
do a good job of ensuring basic services. Securitization of water assets,
raising water prices, and more private-sector involvement in water
supplies are all proposed as solutions.

Singapore's thoroughgoing program of using desalination, rain
harvesting, and water recycling is cited as a model. Using seawater
for some purposes can help. Vincent Bryan De Guia Salvador, 28, the
Philippines, cites UNESCO data that 70 percent of water is used for

agriculture, with about 60 percent of that lost through irrigation. He proposes an alternative:

> With an aeroponic system, only 20 percent of the usual water requirement is used. Being more cost-effective, it also eliminates the need for soil as substrate for planting. This would translate to further reduction in manufacturing and maintenance costs involved in food production while minimizing the conversion of nature reserves into arable lands.

Pricing water is a sensitive issue, and Rohit Honawar, 29, India, is one of the few to embrace it:

> Pricing that does not truly reflect the value of water encourages its inefficient use, and must be reevaluated. . . . It is through the implementation of private–public partnerships and an appreciation of responsibility toward the community that a country can move towards achieving water security.

Park is another who writes of the possibilities of using market-based mechanisms as a solution, citing a report by the Hong Kong–based, nonprofit Association for Sustainable & Responsible Investment in Asia (ASrIA).[8] Park looks to more private-sector investment and the development of capital-market securities linked to water services:

> Securitization of the water sector will expand the market rapidly attracting more investments, which will then increase water quality and provide steady water supply services. However, if the securitization of the water sector is to succeed, domestic debt capital markets should be developed to provide greater liquidity in the market. A legal and regulatory framework should be established to ensure that the credit risks of these securities are properly assessed and the transaction is accurately structured.

Akhilesh Variar, 23, India, also writes about the need for private-sector involvement:

> There needs to be an increased investment in water technology; some, like drip irrigation techniques, have been hailed as tremendous achievements. There should be an emphasis on

increased efficiency of water use. Innovative pricing models and cost reduction must be provided for avenues such as recycled water and desalinization techniques. Businesses need to recognize the importance of water both as life-sustaining and also as an unsurpassed business opportunity.

Food

Food is a daily worry for many Asians. Despite the Green Revolution of the 1960s and 1970s, and the dramatic productivity improvements in rice and other staples that made it possible to feed hundreds of millions more people, Asia has more of the world's poor than any other continent. According to the Food and Agriculture Organization (FAO), Asia is home to about two-thirds of the 1 billion people in the world who don't have enough to eat. UNICEF estimates that more than two-thirds (100 million) of the 146 million underweight children under age five in the developing world live in South and East Asia.[9] Food prices have been on a rollercoaster since 2008, with sharp price increases again in 2011. Decades of underinvestment in agriculture, coupled with demand for more meat and dairy by Chinese and Indian consumers, mean it's likely that food prices will remain on a sustained upward trend.

Asia is among the world's most important food producers, but its large amounts of low-lying land make it especially vulnerable to climate change. Pham Thuy Trang, 26, Vietnam, notes that a substantial portion of the Mekong basin, a granary of global significance, would be flooded if the sea level increases one more meter.

Rashmi Raman, 27, India, laments some of the challenges facing Asian farmers:

Asia has the capacity to be the rice bowl and the wheat granary of the world. Surprisingly, we have not risen to our potential, considering the large number of Asian nations that are agrarian economies. The truth is that most farms in Asian countries are no longer big enough to carry out economically viable farming practices. Farmers with small land holdings are being forced to abandon their traditional occupation because of the lack of viability. Climate change, which is very much in the news these days, brings along prolonged droughts or unseasonal rains and floods that affect farming adversely. The coverage of deserts in Asia is constantly on the increase, thus decreasing the expanse of fertile land. Is it any surprise then that there is also a tremendous exodus of the rural people to urban areas in search of work that is not subject to the vagaries of nature?

Francis Echon, 27, the Philippines, adds:

In order to protect the remaining agricultural lands, Asian governments should impose prohibitions on converting these lands to nonagricultural purposes. To be able to maximize their potential, governments may initiate extending capital and financial assistance to farmers, so that the latter may cultivate all available farmland with quality crops producing high yields. Modern techniques and equipment should also be made easily available to qualified farmers. Governments have already launched programs intended for farmers, but most of these programs do not reach farmers from far-flung areas, where larger agricultural lands are located.

Given the attention to food security in recent years, the controversial issue of countries buying farmland abroad attracts surprisingly little comment from the essayists. One who supports the concept is Ian Teves Gonzales, 21, the Philippines:

Some countries are offering farmland for lease or sale to foreign investors. Rich-but-food-poor countries are using their money to increase their countries' food supplies by outsourcing food production. Why not make it as a pan-Asian strategy? Instead of being reluctant due to fears of loss of sovereignty or of food crisis in the investee country, one could view it as a win-win solution where agricultural, poor countries could have income through abundant food production, while rich-but-food-poor countries could have food through investments. If managed properly, the food-producing countries would definitely be at surplus production, thereby retaining part of their produce for local consumption.

Higher agricultural productivity is the key to feeding a world whose population is becoming both larger and wealthier. Yet there is little mention of the importance of—or danger from—genetically modified food, and relatively little attention given to productivity improvements. Indeed, the only writer on the issue is Buna Rizal Rachman, 22, Indonesia, on the method of growing rice known as Systems of Rice Intensification (SRI). This farming method is still regarded as unproven but is currently the subject of rigorous testing. Rachman writes:

> SRI is still controversial in some circles, despite our ability—given more space than is available here—to explain in scientific terms why younger and fewer seedlings transplanted with wider spacing and no continuous flooding, and nourished by compost rather than chemical fertilizer, give a much higher yield than conventionally grown rice. By changing how plants, soil, water, and nutrients are managed, SRI can achieve average yields about double the present world average of 3.8 tons per hectare. Since SRI reduces seed requirements by 80 to 90 percent, it slashes otherwise significant hybrid seed costs. Farmers do not need to use chemical fertilizer or other agrochemicals, as the highest yields come with compost made from any available biomass, and SRI-grown plants naturally resist pests and diseases. The most beneficial feature of the SRI method is that it defies the traditional idea that rice can only be grown by irrigation systems that continuously flood. SRI requires less water compared to the traditional method.

Energy

Asia has a serious problem with energy. Outside of the Gulf, only a handful of the region's countries, notably Brunei and Malaysia, are net energy exporters. Energy security has garnered some attention, the dangers posed by climate change far more. There is a broad call among young Asians for financial and technical support in dealing with climate change, but there's no more consensus among essayists than among global climate change negotiators as to how to finance the transition to a sustainable, low-carbon economy.

Naqvi of Pakistan laments that, despite being exposed to the effects of global warming, most people in the region do not have a clear picture of what is happening and how they are contributing. She cites a 2007–2008 Gallup poll conducted in 127 countries on global warming awareness. "A third of people around the world have never heard of global warming. In India it is 35 percent, Pakistan 34 percent, and Bangladesh 33 percent," she writes.

There is also a general desire for a more sustainable economy. Here is a commonly expressed sentiment, by Ronald Decina, 26, the Philippines:

> The solution to this environmental crisis is sustainable economy. Sustainable economy is the process by which governments reshape and refocus their policies, investments, and spending towards clean technologies, renewable energy sources, green transportation and buildings, and sustainable agriculture and forestry. . . . Programs like investing in sustainable agriculture and forestry to replace the natural resources being consumed must be a priority among governments in developing countries.

Renewable energy is an attractive option, and many of our essayists laud its promise, though few of them confront the hard truths of costs—renewable energy typically costs more than fossil fuels and doesn't have the reliability or scale of conventional power plants such as coal.

Naqvi points out that renewable energy is likely to be cost-effective in remote locations:

> Investment should be driven towards solar power, wind farms, biogas, and other means for energy generation. In remote industrial units, solar panels can be a cheaper option than diesel-powered generators and can be used to power small electrical loads up to hundreds of watts. Although the start-up cost is more expensive than a generator, the economics balance

out because there are virtually no running costs. Solar is particularly efficient if site access is difficult as in mountainous areas. While at the moment it cannot compete with conventional power-generation costs, it is closer to the electricity tariff actually charged to residential and industrial consumers since there is no supply cost involved. Precise calculation of solar electricity costs depends on the location and the cost of finance, but in sunny areas such as India and the Middle East, solar can be an effective means of generating electricity. Another alternative is the use of wind turbines. Suzlon, an [India-based] wind-power company that manufactures wind turbines, has installed more than . . . 4,200 MW globally of wind-power generating capacity. Large corporations like Google, which uses wind power in Iowa to operate its huge data centers, use electricity generated by wind. With today's technology, wind is highly efficient, at about a quarter of solar power's cost. Also, wind turbines come in a variety of sizes that can meet the needs of individual households, industries, towns, and villages.

Naqvi goes on to write that Denmark, Spain, and Portugal have proved that wind power can generate electricity on a country-wide basis:

Currently wind meets 20 percent of energy requirements for the former and [more than 15 percent] for the latter two. With no fuel costs and little maintenance charges, in strategic locations the capital and leverage costs become very competitive with other energy sources. To meet its increasing energy requirements without destroying the environment, Asia needs a national renewable-electricity standard that would set a percentage, say 25 percent by 2020, of electricity generated for utilities that would have to come from wind and other renewable energy sources. A heartening sign is usage in India, China, and even Pakistan of power generated by wind. The Director of the Alternative Energy Development Board of Pakistan, Irfan Afzal Mirza, has stated that Pakistan would be able to produce another 1,000 MW of power through wind energy within a few years.

Jain, of India, adds that energy-efficient buildings can be built that have net-zero carbon emissions:

Among the design technologies that can be incorporated are natural day-lighting, glazed windows, rooftop solar-electric cells, natural ventilation, ground source heat pumps, ultra insulation, rooftop solar water and space heaters, waterless urinals, more efficient lighting technologies, and motion sensors for lighting. With buildings accounting for about a third of Asia's energy consumption and greenhouse gas emissions, this could drastically cut down energy consumption.

Finally, Jain advocates replacing conventional grids with smart grids that deliver electricity from suppliers to consumers using two-way digital technology to control appliances at consumers' homes to save energy, reduce cost, and increase reliability and transparency.

Essayists put a great deal of faith in individual efforts, education, and government initiatives to solve energy and environmental problems. Some mentioned the role that the private sector or social enterprises could play. Few mentioned the role that higher prices could play in changing behavior; however, the Clean Development Mechanism (CDM), an effort that tries to mimic the market by putting a price on carbon and thus cut down on greenhouse gas emissions, was mentioned as a way of limiting climate change.

Piyush Panigrahi, 21, India, writes:

Market-based mechanisms to promote energy efficiency and renewable energy, though promising, need to be strengthened. Inferring from activities under the CDM, established by the Kyoto Protocol, market-based mechanisms offering incentives for new investments in renewable energy and energy efficiency may be the best way to boost private investment. However, it highlights the fact that market-based mechanisms excite the private sector only in countries that have achieved a fair degree of economic development. The unequal distribution of CDM projects across countries is due to a lack of developed markets and entrepreneurship in the least-developed countries, and also reflects the inability to develop baseline estimates. It is important to design these mechanisms carefully so that desired activities do not get marginalized. With similar stages of market development and similar technology needs, countries can collaborate in sharing technology experiences in designing and implementing policies. Collaboration could include designing a regional, market-based mechanism for promoting sustainable development, drawing on the lessons learned from the successes and failures of the CDM. A cooperative and collective approach would address energy-related issues and would lead to economic and environmental benefits for the region.

The opportunities of the emerging green economy are there for businesses to seize. Sophie Choi, 22, South Korea, writes:

Big business is more divided on energy and the environment than ever before, and the growing rift reflects major power shifts in the economy. On the one side are business leaders and shareholders who derived their wealth from resource extraction, fossil-fuel-based power generation, and energy-intensive manufacturing—they are the *dirty rich*. On the other [side] are business leaders who run knowledge or service companies that generate very little pollution—the *clean rich*. . . . In other words, the "dirty rich" are dying off, and the "clean rich" are coming of age.

Conclusion

There is a hunger for regional solutions to tackle environmental problems. Asia's various institutions have been of limited effectiveness, especially compared to their European Union counterparts. But young Asians over and over again look for regional solutions. Does this reflect a lack of imagination, a lack of political reality, or a yearning for a more unified Asia? The answer is probably a mixture of the three.

Reuben Andrew Muni, 27, the Philippines, writes:

When one is on board a plane and looks at the land below, one would realize how silly we are in putting artificial markers that we call national boundaries to delineate which is ours and which is not. But nature isn't as silly as we are and does not make boundaries. As a region, Asia is experiencing environmental crises that are mostly trans-border in character. Deforestation, industrial pollution, water crises, and global warming are at the top of the list.

If international leaders cannot solve global problems, Asia should try to work out a regional solution. Dang Thi Phuong Thao, 29, Vietnam, writes:

> The failure of the Copenhagen round of climate negotiations, because of the conflict between the commitments of different continents, somehow strengthens the notion that the environmental issue should be discussed regionally first, as countries in the same region bear the same problems. I suggest a conference in Japan in 2011–2012 in Kyoto for Asian countries to come up with a specific agenda for regional climate change issues.

A similar sentiment is expressed on energy research by Joseph James, 29, India:

> Much of the renewable energy research happens in the United States and Europe, so I would like to see a state-of-the-art renewable research and development center come up in Asia that attracts the best talent from the world and plays a pivotal role in the area of renewable energy research. It is noteworthy to point out that, looking forward, the economic market for green energy will be a huge market, and private players should actively look to tap this market. Alongside, governments should come up with prudent incentivization schemes for green energy that will see substantial outcomes.

Sudhansu Senapati, 29, India, also wants Asia to take more control of its energy future:

> There is a need for an Asian counterpart to the International Energy Agency through cooperation between the Asian Big Four (China, India, Japan, and South Korea) with a view to coordinating long-term, energy-import policies. Apart from political leadership, Asian countries urgently need to establish

an Asian energy grid and an effective collaborative mechanism to secure stable supplies. They also need to obtain lower fuel prices through strong collective bargaining.

Technology can play a role in regional environmental issues, contends Lee Meau Chyuan, 29, Malaysia:

The ability to disseminate information easily and quickly can be used for the benefit of mankind. Although not limited to Asia, one good example for Asia is the Indian Ocean Tsunami Warning System. Following the 2004 Indian Ocean earthquake and tsunami, it was developed with the purpose of sending out warnings to governments of an impending tsunami. In the future, when it is possible to send out warnings to the masses within a short span of time, it would definitely help in saving lives.

On water, too, a regional approach is needed. "There is a pertinent need to develop a dedicated comprehensive regional framework to tackle issues related to water scarcity," writes Variar, from India, citing the Association of Southeast Asian Nations (ASEAN) and the Shanghai Cooperation Organization (SCO) as organizations that might provide support. "The only obstacle would be summoning the political will to do the same." Indeed.

The need for political will is often invoked by essayists, if only to lament its absence. But the hunger for stronger regional solutions on the part of young Asians appears as a leitmotif. As they come into positions of increasing power and influence in the years ahead, the challenge for these young Asians and their peers will be to realize this ambition of a more unified Asia.

Essayists Cited

Introduction
Sibtain Naqvi, 28, Pakistan

Natural Disasters
Eeman Siddiqui-Malik, 27, Pakistan
Sibtain Naqvi, 28, Pakistan

Water
Soyen Park, 25, South Korea
Shreyans Jain, 20, India
Vincent Bryan De Guia Salvador, 28, the Philippines
Rohit Honawar, 29, India
Akhilesh Variar, 23, India

Food
Pham Thuy Trang, 26, Vietnam
Rashmi Raman, 27, India
Francis Echon, 27, the Philippines
Ian Teves Gonzales, 21, the Philippines
Buna Rizal Rachman, 22, Indonesia

Energy
Sibtain Naqvi, 28, Pakistan
Ronald Decina, 26, the Philippines
Shreyans Jain, 20, India
Piyush Panigrahi, 21, India
Sophie Choi, 22, South Korea

Conclusion
Reuben Andrew Muni, 27, the Philippines
Dang Thi Phuong Thao, 29, Vietnam
Joseph James, 29, India
Sudhansu Senapati, 29, India
Lee Meau Chyuan, 29, Malaysia
Akhilesh Variar, 23, India

Chapter 5

Governance

Dig your well before you're thirsty.
—Hindu proverb

Introduction

Protests in Egypt and Tunisia toppled governments and sparked a regional uprising in early 2011; the United States faced the threat of a governmental shutdown as two parties wrangled over the budget; and governments in Europe suffered stinging rebukes from voters as a result of austerity measures. It could be the coincidence of political upheaval in many countries. Or it could be a brewing crisis in global governance.

Asia is not immune to governance challenges. Japan has seen six prime ministers since Junichiro Koizumi stepped down in September

2006. The ruling People's Action Party (PAP) in Singapore saw its share of the popular vote slip to its lowest level in more than four decades in the May 2011 elections. And these are the top two Asian scorers on a popular global governance index.

China continues to be dogged by questions about the growing gap between its economic and social changes and its political rigidity. In India, the media produce a never-ending drumbeat of stories about corruption. Corruption in Indonesia and the Philippines remains rampant. Yet everywhere, it seems, citizens are demanding that governments live up to higher standards.

One common thread linking these very different events is the role played by technology. There is an unprecedented immediacy to news, whether it is unfolding political events in Tahrir Square or an irate Communist Party official berating journalists in China. Whether through YouTube, Twitter, instant messaging, or the Internet, wrongdoings can be exposed instantly—and protestors mobilized almost as quickly. Grassroots critics can find their influence magnified as their opinions go viral.

There are drawbacks in an instant always-on world. Time for fact-checking, let alone reflection, falls victim to the pressure of a never-ending appetite for news.

Yet there is no going back. Political leaders struggle to satisfy the demands of a fickle, insatiable public. Companies face similar challenges. In the 1990s, corporate social responsibility (CSR) meant philanthropy. Today, CSR has been replaced by a trio of issues—environmental, social, and governance (ESG)—and calls for "conscious capitalism." Although companies are focused on profits as never before, the best recognize that they must have a social license to operate. That means a deeper engagement with local communities, more attention to environmental and social factors, and the adherence to a wide range of global standards.

Asia's Tiger Cubs have high demands of their leaders. Their parents hoped for little more than peace and a chance of modest prosperity for those who worked hard. They didn't expect government to be honest; they didn't expect much in the way of free education, let alone generous social services. Corruption and abuse of power too often were tolerated as part of a landscape as old as Asia's paddy fields. The examples of Hong

Kong's Independent Commission Against Corruption (ICAC) and Lee Kuan Yew's Singapore were beacons of probity in a dark night.

Today, much has changed. Both governments and corporations are more responsive and transparent than three decades ago. In many countries freedom of information laws allow greater public scrutiny. But expectations of better governance still outstrip reality.

Many of Asia's Tiger Cubs worry that poor governance may hinder future economic success. Writes Omer Randhawa, 25, Pakistan:

> While the whole world has been fixated over the promising economic indicators and the growth potential of the region, the curse of weak political systems has been consistently ignored. . . . If the very root of the Asian social structure keeps on decaying, the Asian tree would not be able to blossom with economic fruits for long.

These fears are well-founded. The World Bank–backed World Governance Index gives poor marks for many Asian countries in areas ranging from rule of law to peace and security. Asia's history of social hierarchies and economic inequality has contributed to what has been called a dynastic system of governance in South Asia, typically leading to corrupt systems and a deep mistrust of government. Randhawa's home, Pakistan, scores a poor 0.50 on the World Governance Index, near the bottom of the list. The average global score is 0.63; many South Asian countries, including neighboring India and Afghanistan, score well below average.[1]

Countries in the Asia–Pacific region had an average ranking of just 3.7 (where 10 is the best score) on the 2010 Transparency International's Corruption Perceptions Index, an annual scorecard that ranks 178 countries according to the amount of corruption in the public sector. Asia–Pacific countries scored significantly lower than Europe (average of 6.5) and only marginally better than Sub-Saharan Africa (3.2). Within Asia, some of the most rapidly growing nations are also perceived to be extremely corrupt—China scores 3.5, while India scores 3.3.[2]

Improving Asia's systems of governance—both political and corporate—will be essential to ensuring a strong Asia in the next decade. Many young Asians called for more representative governments for their countries and argued for a freer economic market in order to improve transparency and equality. Instituting democracy is not like flicking on a light switch. Democracy requires a host of supporting institutions, from an independent legal system to a free press and well-developed civil society, to be effective.

As young Asians gain more access to social networking and information gathering through the Internet, political activism becomes easier. It is almost certain that demands on governments and corporations will continue to escalate. While some young Asians propose governmental policies and initiatives in order to tackle problems such as social inequality, climate change, and a weak educational system, others complain that the government itself requires reform before other changes can be made. Without effective governance, Asia's continued rapid economic growth could stall out.

Representation

The strongest calls for governmental overhaul come from South Asian countries, where essayists object to corruption in governments, and note that leaders rarely seem to reflect the opinions of the people.

The firm anticorruption standpoint of Generation Y Asians marks a notable departure from their predecessors, who largely viewed corruption as a necessary evil in order to get things done. While a few dollars in the hands of the right people can expedite otherwise-interminable bureaucratic processes, get children into the right schools, or simplify business practices, young Asians express vehement disapproval of corrupt practices.

Young Asians agree that the government itself cannot be trusted to make positive changes to combat issues of misrepresentation and corruption. They propose lessening governmental power through private-sector partnerships, nongovernmental organizations, or international bodies such as the UN as a way to make Asian governments more accountable. Young Asians similarly advocate increasing citizens' voices by empowering specific populations to take a more hands-on approach to government or by increasing the amount of governance at the local and municipal level. Young Asians call for increased transparency and accountability in order to ensure that their leaders represent their best interests. Like many challenges, implementing these changes is easier said than done.

A number of essayists comment on the disconnect between the people and their leaders, citing issues from hereditary politics to special interest groups. Randhawa of Pakistan discusses the issue of representation in his native Pakistan:

> Politics is widely considered one of the most lucrative investments. . . . This is why elections are often engineered by power blocs, so that the power remains within. Extravagant election campaigns are witnessed during the general elections, where the poor sell their votes for a minor incentive. If this "carrot" doesn't bring about the desired results, the "stick" comes into play in the shape of blatant use of state machinery for rigging. Therefore, the politically uneducated masses don't really get to decide for themselves and the electoral system fails to produce true representatives.

Despite the fact that young Asians bemoan this disconnect, some feel optimistic that a rise in civil society in some Asian countries is providing ways for citizens to become more involved in choosing their leaders. S. Nagendra, 31, India, writes:

> There is an increasing trust deficit in leaders and also in political institutions. However, the good news is the growth of civil society in making people more conscious and assertive on issues related to governance. Due to the rise and reach of electronic media and information technology, Asia's societies are throwing up credible leaders from civil society and from the grassroots who are working toward fulfilling the aspirations of the public at large at various levels but are outside of the political governance system of their countries. The problem is that these leaders do not wish or intend to participate in office-occupying governance positions where usually money or muscle power plays a dominating role.

Many young Asians speak of the inaccessibility of governance, and the ways in which certain groups or qualified candidates are excluded from power. Loh Su Hsing, 31, Singapore, a runner-up of the essay contest, is one of the few essayists to touch on the subject of elite governance. She writes:

> From developed countries like Japan to developing countries like Thailand, from democracies like the Philippines to authoritarian regimes like China, most Asian countries continue to be plagued by volatile domestic politics despite economic growth. Such instability can be partially attributed to the fact that Asia leans heavily toward elite governance, which is deeply embedded in Asian culture. It is virtually impossible for unknowns to make their mark. Political leaders are usually descendents of political pedigree or foreign-educated elites.

Nagendra also writes on the theme of inaccessibility, discussing the ways in which those in power fail to represent all citizens. He writes:

> The rise in identity politics is essentially based on social groupings of common cause. The problem is compounded, as most Asian states have even refused to acknowledge the existence of different social groups who lay the foundation of identity politics, let alone deal with them. One of the most simple ways to tackle this problem is by first recognizing and then . . . gradually empowering them. The states, by refusing to accept this social reality, in turn spend huge resources and failed efforts in trying to suppress identity politics. This causes often-violent conflicts.

Nagendra suggests combating identity politics by empowering otherwise-neglected populations:

> If the state spends even a fraction of [its budget] on acknowledging and empowering different social groups, it will most importantly take the "steam" out of identity politics. Empowerment is two-fold—both political and economic—and should mean affirmative action rather than a few employment and reservation measures, so that other groups buy into this idea. Measures like equal political rights, employment equity, skills development, ownership management, socioeconomic development, and preferential procurement are some of the steps in empowerment. The success of the Black Economic

Empowerment program, launched by the South African government to redress the inequalities of apartheid by giving previously disadvantaged groups preferential treatment, holds important lessons for Asia.

Across the board, young Asians concerned with the lack of effective representation advocate a greater role for ordinary citizens in choosing their leaders. In addition to the empowerment of certain identity groups, young Asians suggest increasing involvement on the local and municipal levels in order to give citizens a greater voice in picking their representatives. Nagendra writes:

> To restore credibility in political governance, there has to be a "nondemocratic" way of allowing such credible people of trust and worthiness to occupy positions in political governance structures. This may seem a contradiction of sorts, but it is essential and implementable. Although Sweden is a very different country, a similar architecture in local popular governments has restored the faith of the masses in the political system. This kind of participatory flavor can be brought in by experimenting within local governments like villages, towns, or municipal administrations, which directly impact millions of lives.

Young Asians feel equally strongly about the issue of corruption. Many cite corruption as the underlying cause for a number of social ills in Asian countries, while others fear that continued governmental corruption would lead to anti-governmental protests or violent uprisings. Rohit Pathak, 20, India, an essay contest runner-up, underlines the need for strong and trustworthy governance in Asia:

> Without good governance, all policies, plans, or solutions are redundant. The biggest hurdle in the way of good governance is corruption, as it is, undoubtedly, the direct and indirect cause of almost the entire spectrum of our problems such as poverty, terrorism, illiteracy, poor infrastructure, and others, which probably, in its absence, could have been solved by now. On the domestic level, therefore, besides increasing the efficiency of our countries' government machinery, our primary aim must be to

develop an effective framework for tackling the governmental menace of corruption.

Young Asians advocate increasing transparency of governing institutions in order to address the issue of corruption, presenting both information technology and international organizations as potential avenues toward greater accountability. They supported an increased role for international organizations in monitoring and preventing corruption, calling for a pan-Asian entity to police wayward governments, and more regulatory measures from the UN.

Despite the fact that other attempts at regional integration, such as the European Union, have been accused of inefficiency at best and corruption at worst, many young Asians look outside of their domestic governments for solutions, believing that a regional organization could increase transparency between nations, as well as hold governments accountable to one another. Randhawa writes:

> Therefore, a strong Asian economic and political union is the need of the hour. . . . Only a strong central union could put pressure on the member states to improve their political systems so that the economic gains are widely and wisely distributed among the masses. Naturally, disparities will always remain, but to a minimum threshold so they do not leave a vacuum for extremism, internal uprising, and terrorism.

Other young Asians suggest that, in order to fully remove corruption from government practices, it is necessary to lessen the role of individuals in carrying out government schemes. The most effective efforts would involve reducing government involvement in everyday procedures and practices by using information technology (IT). Young Asians highlight IT's ability to improve transparency and increase civilian involvement in politics. One such solution is set forth by Pathak, who suggests utilizing IT to improve government transparency while simultaneously increasing the reliability of governmental programs:

> The Union Government of India, with its noble intentions of ensuring food security to every citizen below the poverty line,

has a reasonably good policy in place, has considerable funding for the project, and even has a widespread Public Distribution System (PDS) along with an army of bureaucratic workers in villages to ensure the distribution of food grains at the lowest level—all in vain, unfortunately, because of the unredeemed presence of corruption. . . . The wonders of IT can help us . . . in preventing or at least reducing corruption in the first place and at the lowest level where it matters most. . . . Because of the patent failures of the PDS, the Indian Government is already contemplating scrapping the distribution system altogether and is planning to directly give food coupons or cash to families below the poverty line so as to save them the trouble of facing corrupt PDS staff and bureaucrats. . . .

Such a move is welcome, and it gives policy makers enough ground to speculate and plan further. Thus, for instance, to ensure the delivery of these food coupons to [poor farmers], these coupons could be made electronic (say, like a credit card), and could be designed to contain, along with other identification information, accurate biometric details of every person in the family, associating them with the already proposed Unique Identification Number—an ID number along the lines of the Social Security number in the United States. A network of retail stores could then be set up in remote rural areas by private players, replacing the government PDS. Minimizing government-individual interference, the system would require an entitled person to purchase directly from the private retailer in exchange for his coupon, the coupons being allowed, of course, for later reimbursement. The precise biometric data, along with verification at the time of purchase, would also ascertain that the supplies actually go to the families themselves. . . .

Additionally, if this consumer-supplier transaction data . . . is made visible or accessible to the public, then policy experts could also pick up critical patterns that could help them improve upon their existing schemes. So basically, with the help of information technology, we can create a transparent and accountable system that will "accurately" deliver.

Other solutions center on the idea of reducing the power of corrupt governments by increasing the role of private organizations in government-run programs, such as the food distribution scheme mentioned above. Anish Gupta, 26, India, writes:

> Accountability, participation, predictability, and transparency need to be ensured in framing every policy. Achieving the efficiency of public institutions and delivery mechanisms by containing corruption can be done by forming public-private partnerships and shedding some public work to private parties.

Young Asians present solutions to misrepresentation and corruption that come from a number of different avenues spanning both the public and private sector. They have taken a stand against the idea of a government that does not have the interests of its people at heart.

Private Sector

The themes of equality, transparency, and the pursuit of the public good do not solely apply to issues of political governance. Many young Asians call these aspects of the private sector into question as well, linking better corporate governance to a more competitive and profitable private sector in Asia.

The Asian landscape is changing. Young Asian thinkers express concerns that the current ways of conducting business are no longer relevant, as the world becomes increasingly globalized with the further penetration of IT, supply chains, and multinational corporations. As more of Asia becomes dependent on the global market, young Asians support a shift toward a more market-oriented Asia. They also demand that corporations be made more accountable to society as a whole, adhering to international regulatory and transparency standards.

Young Asian thinkers turn to the government to both encourage and regulate the free market, calling for a shift toward market-friendly policies and initiatives. By implementing a strong regulatory framework, creating incentives, encouraging IT development, and adopting global standards, Asian countries can move away from an overreliance on low-end manufacturing to a higher spot on the value chain.

Aurodeep Nandi, 24, India, looks at a *kulfi* (ice cream) shop in his home town of Mumbai to illustrate the benefits of competition for economic growth. He writes:

Opposite Mumbai's famed Marine Drive (the waterfront over-looking the Arabian Sea), there's a modest shop whose delicious *kulfis* have catapulted it to considerable local fame. The shop itself is the quintessence of India's service sector prowess. Most of the customers come in cars, which in the absence of any special parking space have to be parked on the side of the busy road. In bustling evening hours, you might be forced to park your car several hundred meters away from the shop. While you are wondering at the sheer futility of getting a *kulfi* from your odd geographical coordinates, a man in an untucked shirt briskly runs to your car, beats the glass pane and says, "Kya chaiye, saab?" (*What would you like, sir?*). He makes a mental note of the different flavors you order from the soiled menu card, runs back, and in roughly five minutes gets you the *kulfis*.

You finish your *kulfi,* and somebody in the car obliges by taking the initiative to return the plates and settle the bill. Right when that somebody tries to push open the car-door, another assistant from the shop comes running. He calls out to the first guy who is now taking orders elsewhere, stares for a fraction of a second into space, calculates the bill, and the entire transaction is settled without you having to leave your car. Tissues? The man again sprints back to the shop and returns back with a bunch of them.

Too magnanimous for a *kulfi* worth roughly half a dollar? Not if you consider the several other *kulfi* shops in a half-kilometer radius that are trying to gnaw at the market share employing the same amount of people ready to drag red carpets to car doors. The government has also allowed a Baskin-Robbins to set up shop at the end of the road, causing the local *kulfi* store to compete with a foreign brand. The *kulfi* store had simply risen to the competition.

I am sure that given the gustatory ardor of Asians, street-side eateries in most of the food districts would be sporting similar efficacy. But the difference in the case of India is that the same fundamentals also apply to the rest of the service sector, like IT, telecom, retail, banks, or financial services. The tenets are quite simple. Promote competition, relax regulatory red tape, decrease government involvement and allow more foreign direct investment in services.

As Asians, we react quite well to competition. Protectionism on the other hand, breeds inefficiency. At the core of the problem is perhaps the disincentive of Asian economies to reinvent the services sector given that they [are] nations full of already-profitable manufacturing behemoths.

As foreign competition brings with it myriad economic opportunities, young Asians advocate different methods to better promote free markets and economic growth. Writes Aprakrita Shankar Narayanan, 16, India:

> It is crystal clear that for progress to be made, the economic system we follow has to be capitalism. No other system has demonstrated during the course of human history the same ability to remove poverty and improve the lot of mankind as free markets and capitalism. No other system incentivizes tireless hard work and rewards creativity and resourcefulness as well as free markets.

However, encouraging this kind of market development can be challenging in Asian economies where governments play an active role in regulating business operations. Young Asian thinkers say that the change can come from the government itself, suggesting a shift in governmental policy toward one that encourages the development of free markets. Gupta of India states that private development can be encouraged through governmental incentives, suggesting:

> To catalyze growth, efforts should be made to promote the private sector in the region. Foreign investments have the capacity and capability to plug infrastructure deficits and promote competitiveness. Private investments should be made more effective in the region by ensuring risk mitigation guarantees,

credit enhancements, and development of innovative financial instruments. A well-coordinated public–private partnership along with simplification of tax structures would go long way in sustaining private-sector-led growth in the region.

In addition to government incentives to encourage growth, it is necessary to install a strong regulatory framework in order to manage that growth. Because many countries in Asia are lacking this type of regulation, implementing such a framework is among the first steps a nation can take in moving toward a freer market system and ensuring that it will be governed effectively. Narayanan writes:

> It is very evident from the events of the last two years that a robust regulatory framework is a must for a successful free market economy. Asian countries should take care while building the framework. . . . A robust banking system is vital for any free market to function. A rogue operator in a free market can be a risk for all. The failure of Bear Stearns, Lehman Brothers, and AIG roiled the world markets and nearly created a repeat of the crash of 1929 and the Great Depression that followed. The key for the success of free markets in Asian countries would be their ability to build institutions that create a regulatory framework that will let free enterprise thrive without hindrance but at the same time is alert to systemic risks. Whether it is ensuring that banks are well-capitalized, or securities laws are followed, or predatory lending practices are not allowed, or price-gouging is prevented, regulators are the referees of the free market system who ensure that the system is fair.

Strong incentives and regulatory frameworks would help to encourage free-market activity in Asian countries. Once in place, however, Asian economies must find their own niches within the current global market, essayists note, citing the position of many Asian countries as basic manufacturers as an obstacle to further economic growth. If Asian countries wish for their markets to continue to develop, it is necessary for them to break into opportunities outside of the standard manufacturing supply chain. Many young Asians see the Internet as the solution, encouraging governments and businesses to look toward information technology and the digital media as Asia's next big market.

Lee Meau Chyuan, 29, Malaysia, argues that targeting the online market will grow the Asian private sector, suggesting:

> It seems that it is easier to start a business in the digital age, when anyone can start an e-commerce site or e-business with relatively low costs or even for free. . . . Business will need to have strategies in both online and offline marketing, advertising in almost all major sites or information distribution channels. . . . If there will be more online business and the competition is going to be tougher, the question would then be on how we could promote the growth of more Asian web start-ups. Instead of being the consumer of latest technology or the upcoming web trend, Asia should strive to develop something of its very own. Technology is not meant only for developed nations. Asia would benefit as a whole from regional cooperation with China to develop and fund startups that have been identified with a high probability of success. Success stories and strategies from China such as those from Alibaba and Baidu can also be shared among Asian nations. It is high time that Asians work together to provide a full digital package (take Google TV as an example) in the next decade of information overload. . . . Opening up the China market to other Asian countries will benefit Asia as a whole so that the flow of information and business transactions are healthy within Asia.

Young Asians also suggest that the adoption of international standards would open up many markets for Asian countries, thereby allowing a freer flow of information and capital. Doing so would not only increase Asian competitiveness, but also further encourage corporations to adhere to global standards and governing practices. Yassif Nagim, 29, Malaysia, cites the example of Intel, whose chips have established industry standards, allowing computer makers to design their machines without compatibility issues and earning enormous profits for the California-based company. He writes:

> The first thing that needs to happen is for Asia to start adopting standards. It is a boring and unimaginative way of moving Asia up the value chain but it is a fundamental change that needs to happen. In order to sell to European and U.S. food markets, Asian producers need to subscribe to the standards imposed by the West. Farmers need to observe best practices in how to produce food that is free of diseases and bacteria.

Young Asians emphasize that in order to be competitive in the global marketplace, Asian businesses must conform to a set of international business standards, the adoption of which would increase investment and capital to Asia and allow Asian markets to interact directly and efficiently with the rest of the world's developed markets. Tomoko Nishigori, 25, Japan, writes:

> An issue I think is important for the development of Asia is the introduction of global business common standards, such as the concept of [rule of] law and so on. Hong Kong and Singapore have already adopted these standards, as they have had numerous business relationships with large and global enterprises from other advanced countries in their process of development as financial centers. However, even in some already-developed parts of Asia such as Japan, and key cities of advancing countries such as Shanghai, there still needs to be progress in this area. . . . In order to mitigate business risks and in order for companies to compete more in the global economy, introducing global business standards is important. The adoption of international standards would allow Asia to participate more actively within the global marketplace, and would create growth opportunities and increased investment for many Asian businesses.

Young Asians suggest that governmental regulation of corporations might be problematic due to corruption in the government. Citing "crony capitalism," young Asian thinkers worry that government officials would act in their own self-interests when regulating corporations. Shankar Narayanan writes:

> It is important in countries like India for capitalism and free-markets to take root and survive the bumps along the way [so] that the system is seen as fair. Crony capitalism is the single biggest threat to free markets.

This fear of corruption leads essayists to recommend an outside body to monitor corporations and ensure that they are working in the interest of the public good. Liu Mengyue, 27, China, writes:

> As a moral practice of profitable organizations, CSR can hardly be urged by political coercion or by the consciences of corporations. It needs various NGOs or NPOs [non-profit organizations], which can spur corporations to CSR by negotiation. Therefore, the duty of government is not to supervise CSR directly, but to make public policy that is encouraging for NGOs and NPOs.

Today's young Asians have a real stake in Asia's increasing role in the global economy—they want to see the region develop and prosper, and they want to be a part of it. Their calls for capitalism are supplemented with the idea that corporations should use their new role to contribute meaningfully to the community, and such growth cannot be accomplished without effective regulatory infrastructure and the adoption of global standards.

Conclusion

Young Asians are concerned that Asia's governing practices are too weak, too corrupt, or too underdeveloped to properly manage Asia's rapid expansion. From governments that cannot successfully provide food to rural citizens, to corporations that disregard the environment, the problems with governance in Asia continue to exacerbate problems in the region.

Commercial interests must find themselves accountable to the public, pursuing the common good while pursuing profits. With increased regulations and monitoring bodies in place, such accountability will help to create strong corporations throughout Asia that are part of their communities, in addition to being part of the global business scene.

With young Asians demanding more transparency and efficiency, governments and corporations are becoming increasingly accountable to the people of the region. Young Asians want to see leaders who truly represent them and the interests of their community. They see advances in technology as an opportunity to improve the quality of the region's governance—from digitizing governmental food distribution programs to encouraging civil engagement, the new generation is seeking ways to take today's circumstances and turn them into tools. This generation wants a voice.

Essayists Cited

Introduction
Omer Randhawa, 25, Pakistan

Representation
Omer Randhawa, 25, Pakistan
S. Nagendra, 31, India
Loh Su Hsing, 31, Singapore
Rohit Pathak, 20, India
Anish Gupta, 26, India

Private Sector
Aurodeep Nandi, 24, India
Aprakrita Shankar Narayanan, 16, India
Anish Gupta, 26, India
Lee Meau Chyuan, 29, Malaysia
Yassif Nagim, 29, Malaysia
Tomoko Nishigori, 25, Japan
Liu Mengyue, 27, China

Chapter 6

Geopolitics

If the roots are not pulled out, weeds will grow again when the spring winds blow.

— Chinese proverb

Introduction

Asia's Challenge 2020 essayists see an Asia on the rise. The Tiger Cubs write of an Asia that is decoupling from the West, an Asia in which China stands above all others, and an Asia that is rich and secure. They write of the Asian Century, the rise of Asia on the global stage led by China and India. Theirs is a story of power reclaimed, of an Asia ascendant after centuries of weakness, defeat, and subjugation.

But despite an implicit belief by many that Asia's ascent is unstoppable, writers have not shied away from the region's many problems. Regional wars, terrorism, and other forms of violence top the list of geopolitical concerns. Another worry is how the inevitable tensions will play out among more muscular and self-assertive nations, whether in resource conflicts or more old-fashioned wars of sovereignty. One nation's proud and long-overdue rise is another's nation's cause for worry. Essayists from around the region are concerned about how the rise of China will play out.

Our contest took place at a time of fast-moving events with significant long-term implications. During the 12-week contest period came the announcement that China had overtaken Japan as the world's second-largest economy. The United States continued its struggle to recover from a financial crisis that had prompted a severe recession. Also during the contest period, the euro was buffeted as never before by crises in Greece and Ireland.

Meanwhile, Asia seemed to shrug off the crisis, as China, India, and many other countries powered ahead to chalk up economic growth on a par with the pre-crisis years. To many Tiger Cubs, the West seems tired, dispirited, and in many cases all too ready to cede the baton of leadership to the rising might of the East. "The process of power shift from West to East will mark the new era of power balance where smaller countries have a better chance to safeguard their interests," writes Abdullah Ansari, 24, Pakistan. "The emergence of more power centers will dilute the strength of existing power centers."

A particularly powerful essay by Loh Su Hsing, 31, Singapore, discussed Asia's decoupling from the West. "Asia should decouple from the West, and this process of decoupling will be the greatest challenge that Asia will face in the coming decade," writes Loh.

Chinese Dominance

Many essayists focus on the implications of China's growth. For some it is a source of worry; predictions of tension between China and the United States or China and India are common. So, too, is broader concern about what the rise of China means for its neighbors.

Jesslyn Zeng, 15, Singapore, is among many who take a cautious view of China's rise:

Whilst many Asian countries perceive China's rapid rise as a blessing, one must note how the rise of China may pose many significant challenges to Asian and Western countries. For a start, one must bring China's political reputation into the picture. It maintains relatively close ties with rogue countries such as North Korea and continually contests for monopolization of the South China Sea. China's massive investment in Africa has even been deemed by some as neocolonialism. Putting into perspective the way Chinese officials dealt with Dalai Lama loyalists and China's massive strengthening of military power, countries cannot assume that China would be as benign a superpower as the United States in its friendlier days.

Zeng worries that China could try to enforce its norms in the region:

The rise of China makes tomorrow's world very uncertain. Although China rises to power using Western-like market strategies, China may implement its own version of an economic system when she rises to the top. Will "freedom" not be an enshrined value—replaced with other values such as compliance and obedience? Will the next generation of Chinese think differently from the older Chinese?

From South Korea, Kim Min-ji, 19, also expresses unease about China:

Countries are more nervous about China's military power because China is one of the five permanent members of the United Nations Security Council, and it's legally allowed to possess nuclear weapons. This kind of weaponized competitive atmosphere can never be called "peaceful."

A more muted sense of concern is shown by Ansari of Pakistan:

China's capability to claim the throne of the world is a question mark. In the first place, China as a nation . . . has not tasted the glory of being a superpower. The will and zeal that can be found in other nations of the world like Germany, France, and Turkey, where people always remind themselves of their glory, seems missing in Chinese people. Secondly, China's policies are more region-centric. For example, it has a defined policy for Pakistan and India, but the same is not the case for Africa.

In world issues like the U.S. invasion of Afghanistan, which
is clearly a threat to Chinese interests in the region, there was
not a decisive and bold reaction from China. With a growing economy, China's energy needs are increasing, and, unlike
Russia, it does not have enough resources of its own. As a
result, it has to [develop] close relations with world powers like
the United States.

Ansari's relative optimism notwithstanding, relations between China
and the United States, arguably the most important bilateral relationship
in the world, remain troubled. Relations between China and India also
concern Ansari. "With the growing economies of India and China,
there will be a competition between these two emerging powers to
dominate the global landscape," he writes. "Whichever country identifies
her potential earlier will become a world leader."

Other writers are more optimistic about the role China can play.
Omer Randhawa, 25, Pakistan, writes:

China's recent experiment of the Asian model of development
in Africa could be used as a powerful precedent. In the last
few years, China has spent billions of dollars in the least stable
countries of Africa in the role of infrastructure development.
The ambition, speed, and scale of involvement in Africa are
extraordinary, and yet the Chinese companies seem very risk-
happy. Although China receives billions of dollars of conces-
sions to mine minerals essential to its growing industries, it is
the first time African countries are profiting from their resources.
Another major advantage is the fast pace of the discussion and
negotiation process. While loan talks with multilateral agencies take years, a $5 billion China-Angola deal discussion
[in 2007] took only weeks. The same model of development
could do wonders in Asia. Connecting mineral- and petro-
rich Iran, Afghanistan, the Middle East, and Central Asia with
the energy-hungry states of China and India is the need of the
hour. In return for the energy supplies, India, China, and other
East Asian countries could carry out infrastructure development in the backward regions of Iran, Afghanistan, and Central
Asia. Universities, rail and road networks, hospitals, and health

centers can trigger massive opportunities for the region and improve social indicators.

Zeng, despite the misgivings noted above, offers some ideas on how China might move ahead:

> The key would lie in a very capable Chinese leadership— capable not only in terms of imposing authoritative demands, but also more importantly, winning the respect of the Chinese and their surrounding neighbors. Respect, not coercion, should be guaranteed. Negotiation, and not imposition, should be encouraged. Corruption from the highest to the lowest ranks must be abolished. Transparency should increase, and projects should not be awarded based on membership in the Communist Party but through a fair and just meritocratic system. Sound monetary and financial policies must be adjusted to suit China's growth, and the productivity of Chinese workers must increase. Cheaper labor may be delegated to surrounding under-developed countries such as Vietnam whilst China grooms a more dynamic and innovative workforce. But this may not come easily to Chinese officials, with many conservatives holding major reins in the Chinese government.

Zeng sounds a warning. For all the fears of China, "the greatest nightmare will not come if China rises but if China does not rise." A weakened, fractured China is in no one's interest. The cost would be incalculable, both for China and for the region.

Regional Conflict

Despite the steady rise of Asia, the region is also home to many long-running conflicts. Our essayists wrote of their concerns over violence, ranging from wars to civil insurgencies to terrorism. Most notably, the war in Afghanistan continues, and the lack of clear political solutions is of concern to our essayists. Parkash Kumar Rajasekaran, 17, Malaysia, writes of "a general deadlock with no sides making visible progress."

The longstanding India–Pakistan tension shows no sign of easing. In the northeastern corner of the continent, an uneasy ceasefire has prevailed in the Korean Peninsula for nearly six decades. And Asia is home to myriad local rebellions of varying intensity, notably in India. China has problems with simmering independence movements in Tibet and Xinjiang. The Philippines and Thailand also have Muslim insurgencies.

Some young Asians display deep animosity toward other countries and other religions. Among many strongly held views toward other groups, here are the opinions of Vincent Franklin Velasquez, 31, the Philippines:

> China sees torture as justifiable despite persistent opposition from the international community. The Chinese government is addicted to hunting down political dissenters, from the press to Internet bloggers. China hurts its people in championing the honor of the state, while terrorists will die to kill others. Like social deviants, they flout the norms of society, the global society. Al-Qaeda cannot see the wrong in killing the innocent in the name of God. They distrust others and misconstrue the conduct of liberal societies as malevolent. . . . Akin to delusions, their beliefs are unyielding to logic and intrusive on their consciousness, ruling their actions. . . . Lastly, their conduct is destructive to themselves and others.

Terrorism is the single biggest worry among writers on geopolitical issues, including Vishwanath Praveen, 24, India. He laments the corrupt, ineffective law enforcement officials who allow terrorism to flourish. "Society has created a Frankenstein," he writes. Globalization makes the threat greater. What's new is not terrorism, but the international links between terrorists adept at using the tools of globalization—whether it be laundering money through the international financial system or taking advantage of the ease of travel to engage in human trafficking. Praveen continues:

> Terrorism is not new in East and South Asia. The new twist in the tale is the growing virulence and connections the terror groups have with far-away terror organizations like Al-Qaeda, the Taliban, and some groups from Central Asia. These groups stand out clearly as the mentor for fringe groups, and they pose the No. 1 worrisome factor, especially to Asia. With some

South Asian nations having loose and asymmetrical banking systems, it has become easy to launder ill-gotten money. This alone provides the critical financial base for terror organizations. . . . Catalyzing terrorism's growth are human smuggling and passport fraud, narcotics trafficking, and money laundering. This is the foundation on which terror groups multiply, recruit, assemble, train, and unleash.

One analyst has noted that the Afghanistan–Pakistan region contains what is possibly the largest concentration of weapons anywhere in the world that has not been produced locally. It is estimated that more than 7 million assault weapons are "on the loose in South Asia."

Far from the terrorism of South and West Asia, Kim of South Korea worries that conflict could become even more serious in the future, particularly as a result of an arms buildup in Northeast Asia:

It is undeniable that Asia's strong nations including China, Japan, Korea, and others are strengthening their military powers. Some might argue that this is nothing to worry about because they will never use the weapons against each other, since if a war breaks out, they have so much to lose. However, I see it differently. Imagine a person sitting around a table with others that have their own guns [pointing] towards each other. North Korea is putting its best effort into making nuclear weapons, even though it is not allowed to, in order to demonstrate its power in international society. Not only North Korea but also India and Pakistan illegally possess nuclear weapons.

The key to solving terrorism, young Asians say, is better governance and more economic opportunity. Praveen writes: "The biggest challenge that has to be taken up is the cancer of corruption in South Asia. Corruption and terrorism can be labeled as twin evils."

S. Nagendra, 31, India, looks at the interplay between terrorism, governance, and economic opportunity:

This resurgence of identity and its subsequent manifestation in conflicts can be attributed to the nonfulfillment of social aspirations in the governance system of the state. A study by MICROCON ("A Micro-Level Analysis of Violent Conflict"), a five-year research program funded by the European Commission, which takes an innovative micro-level, multidisciplinary approach to the study of the conflict cycle, found that the level of household participation at the start of and during a conflict is a function of two interdependent variables, namely household vulnerability to poverty and household vulnerability to violence.[1] The poorer the household is at the start of a conflict, the higher the probability of the household participating and supporting an armed group. For example, at least two separate studies that have analyzed the determinants of the intensity of conflict across Nepal's districts have uncovered a possible role for social and economic inequalities in explaining why some districts have been more adversely affected by conflict than others. One study, for example, found that a lack of economic opportunities (measured in terms of higher poverty rates or lower literacy rates) is significantly associated with a higher intensity of violent conflict. In particular, the study suggests that a 10 percent increase in poverty is associated with 23 to 25 additional conflict-related deaths.

Decoupling from the West

Most of our essayists take Asia's rise as a fact. Fast economic growth rates and large populations mean that China and India already place among the world's largest economies. One essayist who tackled the implications of Asia's increasing importance is Loh, of Singapore. She writes:

> [Decoupling is] the overarching process whereby Asia *explores, diversifies, and reduces general reliance on the West.* The key is to engage and cooperate with the West but allow more room for Asia to find its own niche and maximize its potential. It is not a zero-sum game, and it is certainly not about disengaging from the West or isolating Asia.

Decoupling for Asia, says Loh, is less about a break from the West than about the need to find new sources of growth in the region:

> Much has been written about finding the "Asian Way," but this is very much a misnomer, and the concept remains nebulous. The truth of the matter is, nothing in this globalized and interdependent world is completely unique these days, and what we have are merely adaptations and improvements. What is suggested here is *not* a singularly Asian or "un-Western" way, but rather adaptations, improvements, and leapfrogging from what is already in existence. . . . Decoupling is generally perceived negatively, and it is indeed a delicate balance. The key is not to disengage, but to reduce reliance, diversify, and find Asia's niche and optimality. It is important not to alienate the West in the process. The rapid growth in intra-regional trade (which now accounts for more than 50 percent of trade in Asia, according to the IMF), the formation of regional organizations like ASEAN and its affiliated organizations, the calls for the formation of an East Asian community, and the reduced reliance on foreign capital have triggered fears of the formation of an Asian bloc, designed to keep out the West. This should not be the intent of Asia, and to fuel such a perception would be counter-productive—Asia needs the West and vice versa.

Asians often still feel that they are pushed into submission by Western countries. This does not necessarily mean physical or military defeat, but a sort of existential subjugation. The response in some cases is what might seem like misplaced admiration for international pariahs such as Iran and North Korea, simply because they stand up to the West. Ansari of Pakistan worries:

> This submission [of Asia to the West] doesn't mean physical submission or military defeat, rather it's about the dominance of the West in the economic policies and strategic decisions of Asian countries. Even an economic giant like China is unable to enjoy the same privilege on the international canvas as the United States. Rapidly developing nations like India still have a

long way to go to prove themselves to be world powers. Previous world leaders in the Eastern Bloc are not capable enough to regain their influence. Happily, there are signs that some Asian countries are trying to take the initiative, like North Korea and Iran fighting for their right to use nuclear energy solely for their own defense and for technological advancements in energy generation.

Conclusion

How far the thoughts and ideas of this chapter are realized will determine much of Asia's future over the next decade. Some of the ideas are outlandish and even wrongheaded. But it is clear that there is a hunger among young Asians for a more peaceful and a more integrated region.

China is seen by the Tiger Cubs as the key to regional peace and prosperity—but they are not clear whether China's rise is to be applauded, feared, or both. Terrorism and a variety of conflicts continue to tear apart the region and these remain a key area of concern. In most of the cases young Asians cite, there is little hope of any quick end to this simmering violence. Whether international organizations will be able help in this regard is debatable—after all, Asia already has an alphabet soup of organizations concerned with just about every aspect of life, from health to the environment, and from anti-poverty efforts to trade. If this is to be Asia's century, Asia must enhance its cooperation on everything from trade routes to regional institutions. Finally, Asia must realize that decoupling from the West will not mean divorce. But Tiger Cubs think that a more prosperous, more confident, and more secure Asia can and must start charting its own course.

Essayists Cited

Introduction
Abdullah Ansari, 24, Pakistan
Loh Su Hsing, 31, Singapore

Chinese Dominance
Jesslyn Zeng, 15, Singapore
Kim Min-ji, 19, South Korea
Abdullah Ansari, 24, Pakistan
Omer Randhawa, 25, Pakistan

Regional Conflict
Parkash Kumar Rajasekaran, 17, Malaysia
Vincent Franklin Velasquez, 31, the Philippines
Vishwanath Praveen, 24, India
Kim Min-ji, 19, South Korea
S. Nagendra, 31, India

Decoupling from the West
Loh Su Hsing, 31, Singapore
Abdullah Ansari, 24, Pakistan

Chapter 7

Asian Identity

A single strand of straw cannot sweep dust, but a bundle of straw can.

—Filipino proverb

Introduction

Is there a single Asia? Asia is a diverse region. It is home to the largest number of living languages in the world—more than 2,300 are spoken by at least one speaker as his or her first language. In India, there are 22 official languages and more than 400 others; Indonesia has over 700.[1] Asia is also ethnically diverse. China has 55 officially recognized ethnic minority groups in addition to the Han majority. India has more than 2,000.[2] Christianity, Islam, Hinduism, Buddhism, Taoism, Confucianism, Shintoism, and Sikhism are all major belief systems.

Political systems include constitutional monarchies, one-party states, federal states, liberal democracies, and military dictatorships.

Amid these differences, one common element drawing the region closer has been economic development. Asia's Tiger Cub generation was young during the final years of the Cold War era, when international relations were thawing and the U.S.-dominated, unipolar world emerged. As geopolitical tensions eased, global trade accelerated. In the post–World War II decades up until the 1970s, Japan had been the region's main player in international trade, largely due to the strength of its exports in world markets. Other Asian countries also increased their ties with each other and with the world. One of the early means created to foster Asian integration was the Association of Southeast Asian Nations (ASEAN), which was formed in 1967 as an anti-Communist bulwark, as well as to defuse Indonesian-Malaysian political tensions and strengthen the regional economy.

In the 1960s, Hong Kong, South Korea, Singapore, and Taiwan saw growth accelerate dramatically. The Asia-Pacific Economic Cooperation (APEC) was formed in 1989, furthering economic cooperation among Asia-Pacific economies. Global economic integration continued to make large strides, ultimately leading to the establishment of the World Trade Organization (WTO) in 1995. A further milestone in trade liberalization in Asia came when China joined the WTO in 2001. Since then, bilateral free trade agreements in East Asia have proliferated, from just three in 2000 to almost 50 currently.[3] The world's largest free trade agreement in terms of population—between China and ASEAN—came into effect in 2010.

Economic interdependence goes beyond trade agreements. Many Asian nations rely heavily on their neighbors for access to resources and foreign investment. To take a few examples among many: Singapore imports water from Malaysia, and Japan and China import wood from Malaysia and Indonesia. Japan is the single largest investor in Thailand, while China holds the title for the developing nations of Cambodia and Myanmar.[4]

Noneconomic ties have also flourished. The spread of the Internet, freer travel, the growing trend of Asian students pursuing higher education abroad, the expansion of foreign enterprises into Asia, and the growing number of overseas investments of Asian companies have all strengthened old links and forged new ones.

At the same time that Asia and the world are growing closer, those living in Asia are examining what being Asian means in a globalized, integrated era. For much of the twentieth century, Asian countries were preoccupied with settling major border conflicts, as well as post-colonial disputes. At the turn of this century, Asia has settled most of its existential threats and turned its attention to building itself up economically and politically. It is the first time disparate nations in the same region have had an opportunity to think about a longer project of a collective identity—what it means to be part of something bigger. It is in these times that the Tiger Cubs live, and many of their essays call for greater cooperation to resolve economic, political, immigration, and financial challenges that affect the region.

Simultaneously, young Asians' essays reflect the common, shared elements that bind Asia together as a region. The Tiger Cubs are critical of the negative aspects that they believe economic growth has brought with it, including short-term thinking, materialism, inequalities, and the erosion of moral values. They are hopeful that in the longer term, mindsets can be changed to embrace what they perceive as common values among Asian cultures, including social harmony, morality, and pragmatism.

These various sentiments are perhaps indicative of the Tiger Cub generation's deeper search for what might be called the "Asian soul." They envision an Asia that is more unified and cooperative on a wide-ranging set of issues, and one that shares common values while preserving local differences. While some of the young Asians have idealized notions, the significance of this search is that it has the potential to shape national identities as well as Asia's role as a region.

Regional Integration

Tiger Cubs have identified a number of challenges that have caused friction and prevented unity among Asian countries. First, they are concerned that economic disparities between Asian nations breed resentment. Jan Brian Ano-os, 20, the Philippines, writes:

> On one hand, China has been enjoying [rapid] growth for more than a decade already, which resulted in the country

surpassing Japan as the world's second largest economy, and Japan, despite its occasional slowdowns, still boasts a standard of living that could put even many Western nations to shame; while on the other hand, many Asian countries are still considered only to be a bit ahead of their African counterparts in terms of poverty reduction. . . . It seems that when speaking in terms of development, we can only say "China," "Japan," "Singapore," "India," or "Qatar," but we never talk of Asia as a whole.

Besides unequal rates of growth among countries, sustained political tension and border disputes between certain countries threatening regional peace is another concern. As the following opinions make clear, emotions run high when it comes to cross-border issues. Ankit Singh, 20, India, notes:

Asia is not unified; there is tension between countries. In the decade ahead, with constantly rising tensions between Pakistan, China, and India regarding border disputes, West Asia turmoil, Iran's aggressive stand, and a decades-old standoff on the Korean Peninsula, in a blink, nuclear mushrooms could be blowing up on the Asian landmass. A single unfortunate incident could trigger the destruction of our continent and cause it to plummet back into the dark ages. China sees the USS George Washington in the South China Sea as a threat to itself as it continues to foster ties with North Korea, and to plant its men in Pakistan-occupied Kashmir.

Similarly, Sheraz Zaka, 24, Pakistan, points out a series of such disputes that are barriers to regional harmony, which in turn prevent regional integration:

India is emerging as an economic giant, but it does not enjoy friendly relations with its neighbors Nepal, China, and Pakistan. India and China fought a war in 1962 over the control of their border; it is still at an impasse, although trade between both countries has increased many-fold over the past few years. India and Pakistan also have had embittered relations as the countries have fought wars in 1948, 1965, 1971, and 1999 successively. India and Pakistan have a number of disputes which have remained unresolved. The disputes revolve around control over the Kashmir valley, the Siachen glacier, and the construction of the Baglihar dam, the Kishinganga dam and the Wullar barrage in violation of the Indus water treaty concluded in 1960. Similarly, North Korea and South Korea fought a war in the 1950s, and the enmity between both nations is continuing hitherto. Yet it is a fact that South Korea is an economically developed country with exports worth $365 billion, whereas North Korea is a poor country, and the imposition of economic sanctions after it conducted nuclear tests has further brought aggravating consequences. Its spillover effects have brought tension and a rise of nationalism and jingoism in this volatile region, which is very contagious and heralds deleterious effects on the integration and harmony of this region in the future.

Zheng Zhonggui, 28, China, says that the lack of trust persists even after actual conflict ends. Citing conflicts in the twentieth century between China and Japan, North Korea and South Korea, and India and Pakistan, he says:

We can rebuild the destroyed cities immediately, but we cannot cure the hurt souls in a day. Moreover, the countries that launched the wars did not apologize sincerely, which prevented the sort of reconciliation that occurred in Europe.

One resounding theme among young Asians is the call to put aside differences and become more unified. Singh writes:

The idea is to make Asia an integral part of the future world order in order to enhance its role and increase its contributions in development around the world. Forget the next decade, I believe in the whole next century, Asia has a vital role to play to bring about change, which can be achieved only by unifying, the only and final solution.

Khawaja Ali Zubair, 19, Pakistan, echoes the idea:

Rather than thinking about our own personal domains, it's time to think on a greater scale: the scale of countries, the scale of a continent, marked with its own touch of geo-politicism. It [is] about thinking as a whole—targeting and creating, instead of reviving Asian pride. . . . Our progression should be based on working together, moving forward as one. If a crisis plagues one of us, then there should be no doubt that 20 other Asian nations would stand up to offer the tides of comfort.

A key requirement to foster greater unity is to put aside differences and divisions of the past. Zubair adds:

The need of this decade is to forget cultures, religions, beliefs, bridges, and barriers in favor of geography. Why not cast aside the old history books and focus on writing history, history that we would want our children to read without differentiating between heroes and villains?

Stressing the importance of having a unified vision along with visionary leaders, Sanjana Govindan-Jayadev Nair, 24, India, says:

The future of Asia will depend to a great extent on an Asian grand strategy as opposed to a strategy where individual nations square off against each other. Paramount to Asia assuming its global leadership role is recognizing that a bottom-up, issue-based cooperation can build trust and create substantial social, economic, and political opportunities. . . . That Asia lacks a single political, economic, and cultural leader does not mean that it must lack a single vision. . . . It cannot be overemphasized that no progress can be achieved in Asia without cooperation among nations and creating a shared vision. Asian leaders need to speak the same rhetoric, where Asian values and interests are emphasized as opposed to individual national values and interests. Nations should be unapologetic about their pursuit of a common Asian vision, one which enables developing and developed states to actively participate in creating a common good. Antiquated zero-sum arguments from governments seeking to protect their own interests at the cost of others must be rejected. Leaders should pay much less attention to elites who declare themselves as pro-Western and pro-free market. Instead, policy makers need to maximize strategic partnerships and free themselves from rigid ideological blinkers. Asian partnerships must go beyond economics alone, and focus on developing diplomatic and cultural ties and building human capital. . . . What Asia needs now are visionary policy makers who are willing to invest in the future by building alliances and creating consensus among Asian nations. A unified Asian vision focusing on Asian values and principles but embracing universal humanistic goals is the need of the hour.

How can Asian countries cooperate better and become more unified? Marikit G. Manalang, 26, the Philippines, suggests a shared overarching economic objective:

Asia should set as its shared objective the attainment of *prosperity*. . . . Prosperity is a worthy and appropriate objective because it not only talks about human beings' fundamental needs, such as shelter, food, and education, but also incorporates the idea that people should not be merely surviving but *living*. It takes into account people's state of mind and wellbeing, the need and desire to have a life of stability and peace with the opportunity to do things that give them pleasure and satisfaction, as opposed to making a list of statistical indicators and checking to see if the numbers have gone up or down.

Specifically, a goal could be to help the economic advancement of neighboring countries. Ano-os suggests:

Asian leaders, especially Chinese leaders, have long been touting the idea of creating a new "Silk Road" across Central Asia; and with a very good reason: Central Asia's development is actually an important factor in the development of the poorer regions of its neighboring countries, including western China and southern Russia. . . . Creating an economically stronger Central Asia, therefore, should be counted as among the top priorities of its neighbors.

Others suggest going beyond economic goals. Reymart T. Deligero, 15, the Philippines, says:

There should also be partnerships, not only economic, but also in different areas of development, among different countries, regardless of ideology and economic stability. This allows many ideas, plans, and policies to be shared by different member countries, for them to have equal opportunities of development, and thus to reduce the possibilities of sociopolitical wars in the area.

A number of pan-Asian organizations already seek to foster integration in various areas, as described earlier in the chapter. Young Asians suggest new missions for regional integration bodies, as long as national governments can be persuaded to go along with decision making. These are interesting not because they seem likely to be put into place, but because they express a widespread hope for a more unified region. This yearning could augur well for a new generation of visionary politicians who try to build the architecture for an embryonic Asian Union. Singh writes:

> I propose a body of politicians, academics, and students representing all the Asian countries headquartered in Hong Kong, a city at the center of Asia, at the right location for timely dissemination of resources. The body will be fuelled by annual financial contributions from the member countries in amounts varying in accordance with the economies of the countries. It should be based on the structure of the UN but must be far more flexible in decision making; financial and political discrepancies must be dealt with effectively. It would represent a new order, a unification of Asia where there is a unified intelligence service, a unified anti-terror squad, [and so on].

Ian Teves Gonzales, 21, the Philippines, writes that a pan-Asian organization should ensure "an effective intercultural communication among Asian nations, greater coordination and convergence of macroeconomic policies, and a streamlined financial structure, monitoring, and accountability." He suggests:

> These regional organizations could be integrated into one pan-Asian cooperation organization treating each as a responsibility center. Each responsibility center creates its own policies, but such policies should coincide with the region's overall objectives. Each center will then be assigned to different areas based on

what each country/regional cooperation organization is good at, such as agriculture, research, technology, and security, education and health, finance, trade and industry, culture, ethics, and accountability. Such an organization should not only deal with cross-border treaties and policies on trade and finance, but also the fiscal policies of each member country to ensure that all are in line with the organization's goals and objectives. The leadership should first be given to Singapore, being a center for public policy and good governance. . . . All member countries shall be members of each responsibility center to ensure that everyone is involved in the policy-making of each responsibility center, everyone's opinion is heard, and all sides and concerns are well taken into consideration for every action taken or policy passed.

Kim Min-ji, 19, South Korea, wants to build on ASEAN but with a twist—Singapore would have a leading role in settling regional disputes:

The solution exists in the Association of Southeast Asian Nations (ASEAN)+3. The "+3" indicates three countries: China, Japan, and South Korea. It will be difficult, but in such times of division, the countries have to try hard to gather together even if they don't want to. Also, for India, there is the East Asia Summit that will hold India together. Additionally, for North Korea and for Pakistan, there is the ASEAN Regional Forum. In the ASEAN Regional Forum, there are additional members such as the United States, the European Union, Canada, and Russia. These countries are strong nations that North Korea and Pakistan will not offend easily. ASEAN should stand together and unite as much as possible. Just like the European Union, Asian nations can show great cooperation in terms of economics and politics. Further out, there will be more fields in which to cooperate, such as technology, the environment and more.

The European Union did not come out just in a day. The process of establishing the EU was never easy. And it will be the same with Asia. In the process of gathering up EU members, the most serious problem was that the two strongest nations, France and Germany, wouldn't cooperate. As Europe's history shows, ASEAN needs a mediator nation. The nation has to be peace-oriented and democratic, but also a bit authoritarian-rooted. It has to have a high level of economic development in order to lead the nations to have more economic cooperation. I believe Singapore could do a great job. Singapore is a very rich country that could lead the Asian countries towards more economic collaboration. Other nations could be free from worries of imperialism by Singapore. Also, if other nations help, Singapore could play the first great role as a mediator to strengthen ASEAN's economic connections.

In thinking about the common aspects that can be shared among member nations of a regional union, Tomoko Nishigori, 25, Japan, suggests the adoption of English as a common language, with Singapore being a success case. She writes:

In terms of scholarship and education, the educational system in Singapore is one of the models other Asian countries could pursue and follow as an example. The positive point about Singapore's educational system is that although many Singaporeans speak Chinese or Malay at home, they have developed English as the key language in their education. We may have to consider the fact that Singapore was governed by the United Kingdom, and also that Singapore has a key location in the Asian region (an island country on the southern tip of the Malay Peninsula); therefore citizens are quite used to English as a tool for global communication. Considering the above, Singaporeans have realized that an English education is unmistakably crucial for them to enhance and develop their competitiveness in the world. Malaysia has also implemented English education as one of their policies to enhance their growth. (Malaysia's plan for growth is currently the Wawasan 2020.) There is a large gap between the number of global business opportunities for people capable of using English and for those who are not. Therefore, one of the crucial challenges for all Asian countries is to enforce English usage in their countries. One of the ways to do so is to accelerate interactions between

Asian countries. As for Singapore, the country has a diverse population of Chinese, Malays, Indians, Caucasians, and so on. This is largely due to its crucial location in the Asian region. Countries such as China and Japan are more closed to foreigners; therefore, there are still many people who do not feel the necessity of speaking a language other than their mother tongue. By increasing opportunities to interact with people of other nationalities, more people in these exclusive countries may realize the need to learn the global common language.

A more coordinated immigration policy is also proposed. Govindan-Jayadev Nair writes:

The advantages of a unified approach to immigration in Asia are numerous. One part of Asia is very young, with countries like India boasting of the youngest population in the world. However, in other parts of Asia, issues of falling fertility rates and aging populations have become worrying for governments and policy makers. In such nations, immigrants play an important balancing role. Additionally, immigrants bring foreign languages, food, cultures, and ideas to their new residences, almost always ensuring not only diversity but also prosperity for the host nation.

Khan Asif Azad, 25, India, argues that freer immigration policies will allow for more interaction and skill-sharing between nations, thereby narrowing the growth gap between different countries. He writes:

Institutes and work organizations can agree on more exchange programs for sharing knowledge and skills over boundaries. . . . Countries can work towards easier visa and immigration norms to allow easy movement of people helping tourism and cross-national ties. Forming meaningful blocs that represent interests of the region can be worked out easily to represent views at the international level.

Currently, while some countries are making concerted efforts to attract foreign talent, in most places immigrant workers are able to live permanently in a host country only with difficulty. Taiwan started actively recruiting foreign IT talent almost a decade ago, and welcomed almost 300 high-level personnel in 2007, but workers must live in Taiwan for five years, more than 183 days per year, in order to apply for permanent residence.[5] Similarly, Japan and South Korea have relatively restrictive immigration policies. This proves a sharp contrast from Singapore, which offers easily obtainable workers' permits, permanent residence, and tax breaks for foreign white-collar workers.

Govindan-Jayadev Nair further cites the European Union's commitment to develop a common and coherent immigration policy, using the 2007 Treaty of Lisbon as a takeoff point:

> A unified Asian approach should pursue the vision of overall Asian development as opposed to individualistic visions where individual nations undercut one another for supremacy. The features of such a policy should be founded on both Asian values as well as universal humanitarian goals. While keeping in mind some of the challenges confronting Asian nations with regards to immigration, creating a common Asian asylum policy, laying guidelines for the fair treatment of third country nationals, monitoring immigration flows, and defining a common legal framework for admission should be some of the core objectives of a unified policy. Additionally, governments should focus not only on creating binding agreements, but also on developing alternative approaches to keep migration flows balanced.

Govindan-Jayadev Nair warns, however, of the pitfalls of a single Asian policy:

> Among them, the economic cost stands out clearly. Realistically in times of recession, it is hard for governments to make swift policy changes without it adversely impacting their vote bank. Any policy proposed has to speak to both the destination governments as well as the governments of origin of migrants. In the past, immigration policies have increased stigmatization, criminalized asylum seekers, and led to the violent deportation of immigrants in blatant violation of their human rights. There is no guarantee that a unified Asian policy will be any different,

though building a policy framework of common goods is a positive place to begin a more human approach. Finally, a more meaningful immigration policy and management of migration flows has innumerable benefits, and such a policy will succeed if founded on the principles of inter-governmentalism.

Yet another realm is advancing financial integration. Yushi Tanaka, 31, Japan, thinks that financial integration should be a key goal of an Asian grouping:

> If we have sufficient financial markets and allocate this excess capital in a positive manner for both growth and developing areas which need capital, we may be able to develop Asian products and services that are unique to Asia, or even solve problems such as poverty and crime. So I think one of the most important challenges for Asia is to create a common financial center, independent from that of the West. Two main areas for such integration of financial functions are bond and currency markets. From the issuers' perspective, Asian companies should diversify funding sources not only with banks but also with bond investors, in order to prepare for a potential bank crisis and keep continuous funding sources for growth.

Adopting a common currency will be a key to resolving current monetary challenges, he says:

> To minimize risks, the role of an Asian central treasury institution would be very important. The target unified currency value or unified interest rate would be different for each country. For example, the export-oriented countries such as Japan or South Korea prefer currency depreciation, while the import-oriented countries are afraid of currency depreciation with worries about inflation. The countries with deflation dangers hope for low interest rates to stimulate their economies, while the developing countries hold up the hope of high interest rates to control economic overheating. An Asian central institution has to control those conflicts. The central treasury institution should also have both fiscal policy and monetary policy, unlike the European Central Bank (ECB),

which has only monetary policy while each EU country has its own fiscal policy. Without an agreement in terms of cross-border tax and social security systems such as insurance or pension, financial integration would fail in the case of financial turmoil.

Wang Zhiqian, 27, China, believes that a common currency basket in East Asia is needed. He proposes an Asian Currency Unit (ACU) to evaluate the stability of the currencies of the ASEAN+3 countries (ASEAN plus China, Japan, and South Korea). This currency basket would be used to ensure monetary stability for Asia. He writes:

> It is an undeniable fact that the foreign exchange rate of each country is easily swayed by external circumstances. Within the area of ASEAN+3, the unfavorable influences from outside are considered an obstacle in the process of developing. So it is necessary to eliminate this obstacle for sustaining stable growth in East Asia. In the sense of stabilizing the foreign exchange rate of ASEAN+3, the ACU can be expected to play a considerable role in the process of foreign exchange reform in East Asia.

The Tiger Cubs are confident that these common aspects could serve as building blocks for regional integration. What they see is a future of unity and cooperation among Asian countries, with shared vision, leadership, organization, and a commitment to working together to solve a host of Asia's challenges.

Economic Growth and Asian Values

Besides desiring more regional unity and cooperation, Asia's Tiger Cubs are also concerned about a search for common values. They worry that economic development has led to materialism and an erosion of values. A 2010 online poll by Reuters and opinion research firm Ipsos asked 24,000 people in 23 countries their views about money. The pollsters found that about 80 percent of respondents from South Korea, Japan, China, and India thought that money was more important to them than previously, compared with about 60 percent in the United States and in European countries. The share of Asian respondents who thought money was a sign of success was twice that of other countries. An even higher percentage of those aged below 35 placed more value on money.[6]

There is no doubt that economic growth has improved living standards for many in Asia. But at the same time that Asia is getting wealthier, deep-seated unhappiness remains. Events ranging from worker suicides at Foxconn (Apple's most important manufacturer) factories in China to the protests against free trade in parts of emerging Asia reveal deep dissatisfaction with markets.

Some young Asians fear the detrimental effects of rising materialism, social disconnectedness, and the tendency toward short-term thinking. Some of these concerns are common to youth everywhere. Some of them reflect the feeling of being whipsawed as a result of living through a period of rapid changes. Farooq Jamil Alvi, 29, Pakistan, is concerned that:

> Disconnected people live out a schizophrenic lifestyle devoid of the essential elements of a meaningful existence. They are characterized by the key personality traits of materialism, stubborn individualism, and a blind adherence to a day-to-day lifestyle. They are robotic in their being, limited to a struggle of not thinking outside the norm; they are followers rather than leaders, and if the latter, they are un-inspirational. Their lack of empathy, inwards-looking attitudes, and self-preservationist tendencies limit their contribution to society.

He also laments the rising consumerism that he says is rivaling the West:

> The region now boasts some of the tallest buildings in the world (57 of the world's tallest buildings are in Asia), the tallest Ferris wheel, the biggest casinos, and a developing culture of consumerism that is rivaling the Western nations. This is probably the result of the competition the individual Asian countries are involved in. Out of all these, the rising consumerism epidemic is a direct result of social disconnect and poses the gravest danger to Asian societies.

There is recognition that a focus on short-term growth is sabotaging Asia's long-term development. Liang Jianqiang, 26, China, says:

Short-term utilitarian behaviors and actions spoil the development of many Asian countries. For instance, many provinces in China only focus on the growth of GDP but ignore environmental protection. Consequently, environmental threats bring loss of lives and fiscal cost.

Zofishan Shahid, 22, Pakistan, diagnoses the problem as moral decay:

Asia's biggest problem that impacts other areas and hinders growth is the moral decay in its societies. We are poor, deprived of moral education, and devoid of social values. All efforts at development are futile in a society that is selfish and looks for short-term gains.

What are effective cures for these woes? Young Asians place their confidence in the media and the education system in fostering dialogue and a change in attitudes. Alvi contends:

A workable solution needs to be based on an open and thorough discussion of the issue not only on official platforms but also amongst the common populace. It is the responsibility of the governing bodies to enable free and open debates on this topic. The media plays a central and critical role in this, not simply regurgitating the consequences of the actions of disconnected people but also informing and educating the public as to the underlying issues.

Likewise, Shahid mentions the key role of the media in changing mindsets, especially those of the young generation:

To change the mind-set of an adult and his values will require immense effort, influence and time, but a young mind is empty and vulnerable. Media is one way to change the mindset of a nation. . . . Using this medium that is accessible to both children and adults to teach them the importance of moral education might result in a change. Educating a child does not mean only teaching him his ABCs and 123s. It means telling the child the difference between right and wrong: to speak the truth, never to cheat, to work hard, and to stand up for what is right. If his foundations are strong, he will never waver.

Chim Chamroeun, 29, Cambodia, calls for greater investment in values education both nationwide and throughout the region:

> We tend to focus more on "learning to know" and "learning to do" so that our citizens can survive economically; yet we have forgotten another two major pillars, "learning to live together" and "learning to be" which also need to be strengthened. . . . With values education, people can be oriented in a more positive way.

To encourage people to develop a longer-term vision for their societies, Liang suggests that "we should first invest in education, which plays a key role in changing people's mindsets. Furthermore, we should educate the general public to realize the importance of long-term planning and show them the detrimental effects of short-term planning." However, he is sympathetic that in some communities, "basic needs such as eating and living could not be met. It is difficult to persuade people to give up growing illegal drugs plants which could bring them quick money." He proposes job creation activities by the government, particularly in projects that cater to the longer-term needs of communities, such as environmental protection, public construction, and healthcare.

Another solution is to emphasize the positive and common aspects of Asian values. One aspect is the pursuit of harmony and morality. Liang sees certain Confucian values and also Indian philosophies as useful in providing guidance:

> One impact of China's philosophy on Asian societies is Confucianism, which emphasizes loving one's parents/family and following rules of governance. Although Confucianism seems to serve for the benefit of power groups, it helps build a stable, stratified, and harmonious society. Affected by Confucianism, many East Asian countries (China, South Korea,

Japan, and Singapore) embrace the strong, traditional family-oriented values—individuals act for the benefits of their families. . . . Interestingly, the philosophical thinking of India influences the Asian culture in a quite different perspective. Indian philosophy educates people to pursue quietness, morality, and nonviolence.

Another important aspect of Asian values is an emphasis of pragmatism over orthodoxy. Singh, of India, notes:

The pragmatic mindset of new-age Asian leaders is an advantage over [an] orthodox, rigid Western mentality. Asians constantly adapt and change, exemplifying versatility, a quality that comes naturally as a consequence of being born in a highly populated and competitive continent. And Asian leaders must adhere to that by coming together and forming a unified body.

Underlying these solutions is a belief that Asian countries' institutions, including media, governments, schools, and religious institutions, can slowly shift Asian values. If this kind of idealism can spread among the broader population of young Asians, there is hope that the next generation can develop a set of ideals that shape Asia's future leadership in resolving longer-term challenges.

Preservation of Local Differences

At the same time that young Asians call for a search of common values, some are concerned about the loss of local culture and are passionate about preserving the elements that make countries distinctive.

Young Asians suggest reaching back to Asia's long and rich history, which is often forgotten as countries focus on economic growth. As Gonzales, of the Philippines, asserts, in rather Asia-centric fashion:

When Europe was still fighting off barbarians, expanding its borders, and establishing dominions, Asia was already a progressive region with a sophisticated system of government, a complex structure of society, and advanced technology. When the Americas were still under the tribal rule of natives, Asia already had flourishing trade and widespread commercial activity headed by the Chinese in the east, Indians in the south, and Arabs in the Middle East.

Liang, of China, points out how Western imperialism has influenced Asia:

Many Asian countries and regions, especially East Asia, South Asia, and Southeast Asia, were once partially or completely ruled by Western colonists till the end of World War II. Even after the Asian nationalism movement, imperialism has continued and developed into a new form, which is Western economic and cultural expansion in the East. For instance, a big proportion of the Chinese economy is greatly dependent on technologies and investments from Western corporations. Western cultural symbols, like Hollywood movies and pop songs, share a great part of the entertainment market of the new Asian generation.

Though a number of Asian countries have been subject to Western influence due to their colonial history, Tiger Cub Asians are wary of how globalization and increased Western influence affect their national cultures. Patrina Kaye N. Caceres, 22, the Philippines, fears cultural homogenization and domination:

The problem with having a global culture is that it will be dominated by only one culture; since English is deemed as the global language, then the cultures of English-speaking nations will dominate. When this happens, the cultures of the non-English countries will be at risk of eradication. Though globalization would be beneficial for the countries that depend on international trade for economic stability, these countries' cultures will be highly at risk. For globalization to have only positive effects is like having a coin with the other side erased. Globalization is a two-sided process; there is the good and the bad. It should be our hope that as Asian countries join the bandwagon of globalization, the good will overpower the negative effects.

Caceres's vision of an Asia that successfully integrates with the world yet preserves its local culture looks like this:

Imagine an Asia flourishing in business and commerce but still grounded in good values, colorful traditions, and native customs.

Imagine Asian countries booming in industry without forgetting about the blessings of the land—the sturdy, green trees, plants with flowers of every color, and crops that make every backyard feel like home. Imagine. . . . This is my vision of Asia a decade from now. This vision is the challenge that will be faced by every Asian country in the years to come—globalization without forgetting about the environment, and most especially of nationhood, of cultural identity. Think of a "global (insert the name of the Asian country you are from here)" that does not compromise the local culture and environment. This is my vision. For me, to have this kind of society is the biggest challenge for every Asian nation in the coming decade. I am an Asian. I am a Filipino. I am thinking of a "global Asia that does not compromise culture and the environment." I am thinking of a "global Philippines that does not compromise the local culture and the environment." This is my challenge to every Asian nation: "Think globally, and act locally." We stand at the dawn of a new decade, a bright decade at that, as long as we take the challenge of making Asia a leader in the global race without the side effects.

Specific institutions can be tasked with preserving local culture. Caceres suggests:

Countries should develop an organization that would have to deal with matters of culture. This would be called the Department of Culture or some other name similar to that. The organization would defend, develop, and teach culture; by teaching culture, the people will be reacquainted with their heritage, thus establishing their dignity as a people.

Whereas the Tiger Cubs see English as a necessary common language for Asia, they also want local languages to be emphasized. A key institution for doing so is the school. Caceres adds:

Schools must be the first advocates of the native language, as students spend more time in school than in their homes and the community. I have been a witness of younger kids who would rather speak in English and not our own language. You see, Filipino is the national language of the Philippines, but within its islands, native languages exist. And these are being labeled as mere dialects and not as languages by the very institutions that should be defending them, the schools. It is a sad reality; many more kids would talk to you in English and not even understand our native language of Waray (in Leyte). I am an advocate of the native languages, as our professors in the university encourage us to write literary pieces in the language we are most comfortable with. If my language will be eradicated, so will my culture, and so will my identity. I don't want this to happen. And I will not allow this to happen.

Besides preserving languages, schools at the university level can also serve as knowledge centers. Again, there are suggestions to reach back into Asia's rich history. Singh, of India, suggests:

Research labs need to be set up by the governing body to make Asia the knowledge center of the world again, just like it was for 1,800 years. Ancient civilizations need to be resurrected, like the ancient Chinese civilization and Indian Nalanda University, [one of] the world's oldest universities and the first knowledge-dispensing center on earth. Once again, the time has come for the balance of knowledge to naturally shift to the place where it all began.

Along similar lines, Chomwan Weeraworawit, 29, Thailand, suggests a focus on preserving traditional vocational skills, as Queen Sirikit of Thailand has done:

A research and development center is needed in all these countries, where it works as a resource center, a library as well as a "safehouse," a bank of knowledge where the know-how from small rural villages can be relayed and then noted for future generations.

Conclusion

Asia's Tiger Cubs are attempting to strike a balance between preserving the traditional and embracing the global, between unifying as a region and preserving cultural distinctiveness within countries.

Ultimately, uniting Asia and preserving distinctive cultures may be two sides of the same coin. Sanjana Govindan-Jayadev Nair offers Singapore as an example of how unity and diversity can coexist. She writes, "The search for a common identity might seem futile to some, especially in a continent like Asia, but as Singapore has shown, with the right political will in the right political window, it is possible to find similarity in differences." She quotes former Singaporean President Wee Kim Wee on the need to identify traditional and core values that reflected what Singapore's different ethnic and religious communities had in common and that captured the essence of being a Singaporean. These values included nation before (ethnic) community and society above self, family as the basic unit of society, regard and community support for the individual, consensus instead of contention, and racial and religious harmony. President Wee said, "If over the longer term, Singaporeans become indistinguishable from Americans, British, or Australians, or even worse, become poor imitations of them, we will lose our edge over these Western societies which enables us to hold our own internationally." Whereas the next generation must embrace the changes brought about by globalization, young Asians want to feel a sense of pride about their own countries and about Asia. Characteristics that are unique to Asia, the region, yet common among its constituent countries, will shape the region's identity and its place in the world.

Essayists Cited

Regional Integration
Jan Brian Ano-os, 20, the Philippines
Ankit Singh, 20, India
Sheraz Zaka, 24, Pakistan
Zheng Zhonggui, 28, China
Khawaja Ali Zubair, 19, Pakistan
Sanjana Govindan-Jayadev Nair, 24, India
Marikit G. Manalang, 26, the Philippines
Reymart T. Deligero, 15, the Philippines
Ian Teves Gonzales, 21, the Philippines

Kim Min-ji, 19, South Korea
Tomoko Nishigori, 25, Japan
Khan Asif Azad, 25, India
Yushi Tanaka, 31, Japan
Wang Zhiqian, 27, China

Economic Growth and Asian Values
Farooq Jamil Alvi, 29, Pakistan
Liang Jianqiang, 26, China
Zofishan Shahid, 22, Pakistan
Chim Chamroeun, 29, Cambodia
Ankit Singh, 20, India

Preservation of Local Differences
Ian Teves Gonzales, 21, the Philippines
Liang Jianqiang, 26, China

Conclusion
Sanjana Govindan-Jayadev Nair, 24, India
Patrina Kaye N. Caceres, 22, the Philippines
Ankit Singh, 20, India
Chomwan Weeraworawit, 29, Thailand

Afterword

The Tiger Cubs bring with them a new set of aspirations for Asia.

First, this rising generation is demanding. Whether it's cleaning up the environment or rooting out corruption, reforming healthcare systems or decoupling from the West, young Asians' expectations are high. Businesses and governments ignore these at their peril. As employees, consumers, and citizens, Tiger Cubs are distinct from their predecessors.

Second, and on a closely related note, the Tiger Cubs are wired. Technology empowers them. Technology does not cause social or political or economic change, but it amplifies it. The Internet, Twitter, Facebook, YouTube, and myriad other technologies have sped up the pace of change. For an older generation, these technologies are a novelty. But the members of Generation Y are digital natives, swimming in a sea of ever-changing technology.

The immediacy of technology means that videos of events in remote areas can be literally broadcast around the world within seconds. This puts pressure on governments and companies to be more accountable. There's no more information monopoly. Where censorship does exist, the censors are fighting an increasingly difficult battle.

Third, for better or worse, the Tiger Cubs increasingly think of Asia as a *region*. Their vision goes beyond their borders. Globalization, free trade, and a world open to ideas is their world. So, too, are the regional wars and sectarian violence and terrorism that have played a prominent role in their lives, especially in South and Southeast Asia.

It was not many decades ago that too many Westerners, and not only novelists, would label Asia as unchanging and Asians as fatalistic. Those days are long gone. It is Asians—above all, young Asians—who are optimistic, relentlessly pragmatic, and confident about the future.

Appendix

Winning Essays

I Have a Dollar. My Neighbor Has a Million.

By Sarabjit Singh

The Case of the Old Lady

The old lady walks in with the evening crowd, clutching an old bag that she sets down in the middle of the square. Surrounded by fancy windows promoting sparkling jewelry and diamond brocaded watches, and restaurants that charge more per meal than she spends on her food in a week, she unties her sack of wares and lays them out. Five minutes later, she is sitting on her foldable chair with her arms stretched out in front of her, with two packets of paper tissues at the end of each, quietly beckoning the flowing multitude around her to equip themselves for an unexpected case of a sweaty brow or a running nose.

It is Friday evening in Orchard, Singapore's premier shopping district, and the setting sun is making way for the revelry of yet another weekend. The old lady is beginning her lonely struggle to earn what she will need to feed herself tomorrow. She does not have a pension fund, social security, unemployment insurance or old-age benefits. Fluctuations in her daily earnings matter more to her than the ups and downs of the stock market, and she is probably as disconnected a participant as one can be in the economic juggernaut that Singapore is often spoken of as.

Yet if you could zoom out of this tiny island to gaze across the entire expanse of Asia, you will see that she is not alone. From homeless have-nots huddled together in the cold subways of Seoul, watching the smartly dressed haves hustle from swanky offices to heated homes, to a family of six sheltered in their one room wooden shack, listening to the thundering roar of airplanes landing on the strip beside the world's largest slum in Mumbai—jarring illustrations of social and economic inequality abound across this continent.

In the aftermath of the worst global financial crisis since the Great Depression, pundits in the hallowed financial centers of London and New York speak of Asia as the next success story. "Asian countries have been leading a recovery in the world economy," claims an IMF report.[1] Separately, Mr. Dominique Strauss-Kahn, [former] managing director of the IMF, has remarked that "rapid economic growth has turned the region into a global economic powerhouse . . . Asia's economic weight is on track to grow even larger."[2]

That most emerging economies from the Middle East to the Far East will continue to develop in the coming decades seems to be an inescapable conclusion. What is not guaranteed however is whether the fruits of this almost incontrovertible development will be available to all who dwell in these countries. As Asia has grown, so has an underbelly of penniless paupers. The bulk of Asian countries face a growing impoverished population that does not have any stake in the spoils being flaunted by their rich.

Which brings me to the question of this essay. If there is one challenge above all others that policy makers in the region need to address within the next decade, it is this: rising economic inequality. The only way for countries to ensure that their economic growth is sustainable and remains so through their own future and that of their children is to offer Inclusive Development to their citizens.

Economic Inequality

A new measure of global poverty—the Multidimensional Poverty Index—recently made headlines when it pronounced that "eight Indian states account for more poor people than in the 26 poorest African countries combined."[3] Quite a surprise given the contrast between the images that underprivileged Africa usually conjures—that of parched landscapes and malnourished children—and the beaming headlines Indian businesses generate in the pages of the world's business and financial dailies.

But the least confounded were those living in India itself. There, poverty moves alongside opulence like chocolate in a marble cake. BMWs and Mercedes run over fly-overs that shelter shanty towns and slums. And beggars beseech the drivers and the driven when the same cars stop at the next traffic light. The top 10 percent of India's population possesses 31.1 percent of the country's income, but the lowest 10 percent has access to only 3.6 percent.[4]

The numbers don't get much better if we look across the northern border to the country's larger neighbor. According to a Credit Suisse-sponsored report released earlier this year, the average per-capita income for the richest 10 percent in China is 65 times higher (thrice as compared to even the official estimate) than the bottom 10 percent.[5]

And yet, static snapshots tell only half the story. Bad becomes far more unsettling if it gets worse over time. And that is exactly what's happening with inequality in Asia. The Gini coefficient of income—a commonly used measure of income inequality—for most Asian countries has only gotten worse through the 1990s, as shown in Figure A.1. It isn't quite as much the case of the "rich getting richer and the poor getting poorer" as it is of the "rich getting richer faster than the poor."[6] Nevertheless, worsening inequality does not bode well for many countries riding the waves of economic success in Asia.

A 2007 report by the Asian Development Bank identifies a litany of problems—economic, political, and social—associated with rising inequality.[7] According to the report, in imperfect financial markets—a

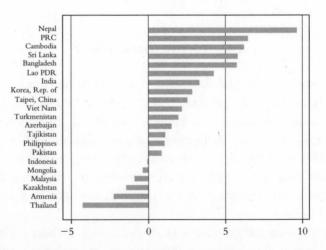

Figure A.1 Changes in Gini Coefficient for Expenditure/Income Distributions, 1990s–2000s (percentage points)[8]

category even the most open of Asian economies belong to—inequality can trap the poor in an inescapable spiral, shutting them out from access to credit, education or business opportunities. To add to this, rising inequality increases pressure to redistribute income, adding potentially distorting mechanisms, and making the markets even less perfect. The report declares that in the long run, "a high level of inequality may actually hinder . . . growth and development prospects."

Of a more immediate worry however, is the report's conclusion that rising inequality can impose tremendous social costs, "ranging from peaceful but prolonged street demonstrations all the way to violent civil war." So even as an economy develops, if it is unable to offer a stake in this development to its poorest, it is only creating a recipe for more social tension. The report quotes a study that "suggests that a 10 percentage point increase in poverty is associated with 23–25 additional conflict-related deaths."

A separate study released last year drew a positive correlation between higher socioeconomic inequality and negative social phenomena such as "shorter life expectancy, higher disease rates, homicide, infant mortality, obesity, teenage pregnancies, emotional depression, and prison population."[9] And if recent events are anything to go by, there is clear evidence that such phenomena related to economic inequality are increasingly taking their toll across the region.

Some commentators have linked the attacks on schoolchildren in China to the rising discontent among its poor and marginalized, "many of whom feel left behind as the rest of China gets wealthier."[10] Similar explanations have been offered for the groundswell of support behind the violence in Thailand [in early 2010]. According to the country's own Ministry of Social Development, the public protests in the nation's capital offered an opportunity to the country's most strapped citizens "to vent their frustrations over declining living standards and the deepening divide between rich and poor."[11]

Biggest Challenge

In breaking down the effects of rising economic inequality, I am perhaps missing out on a slew of others. Nevertheless, it is not the mere number of such repercussions that makes it the most significant challenge facing

Asia today. It is the fact that very high (and rising) levels of inequality can make other problems worse.

To present a few examples, inequality makes it more difficult to address problems of ethnic or religious tensions (socioeconomic disparity has been credited for adding fuel to fire in troubled southern Thailand), or uncontrollable population (rising poverty means more people without access to family planning) or even natural calamities (the greater the number of impoverished, the more the potential victims without the means to prepare for or rescue themselves from floods and earthquakes).

So what then, is the solution? Some economists maintain that rising inequality is merely a stage in the development of any economy. This idea is captured in the Kuznets curve (see Figure A.2). As a country picks up from an initial low level of development, the acquisition of capital adds to the wealth of the new owners of this capital and shows up as rising inequality. Gradually however, redistribution mechanisms restore equality bringing the formerly marginalized sections back into the mainstream economy.

This theory is supported by data from the United States, where the share of wealth held by the top 1 percent of the society grew from 15 percent in 1775 to 45 percent in 1935, before falling back through the 1970s.[12] It could be that Deng Xiaoping had his one eye on these numbers when the then Communist Party leader launched market reforms in China in the 1970s with the famous words "Let some get rich first,"[13] conceivably with the unspoken assumption that the rest will follow later.

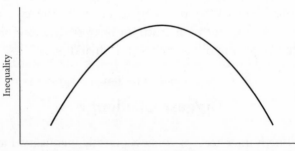

Figure A.2   Kuznets Curve[14]

What worked for America cannot however be expected to work in Asia as well. This region is different; many developing countries here are more densely populated, which means that there are more poor who can band together in groups of sizeable clout, or be brought together by political parties with populist agendas, to demand immediate action. In addition, the times have changed. With technology now connecting previously far-flung regions of a country, the underprivileged can now more easily gape at the affluence of their fellow countrymen, potentially inflaming their grievances even further.

Misguided Solutions

Waiting patiently therefore, for things to take their natural course as predicted by debatable economic theory, is not an option. Before discussing whether an alternative, affirmative approach can make a difference however, it will be helpful to take a detour and briefly look at the underlying causes of economic inequality.

The ADB report quoted earlier claims that worsening inequality limits the poverty alleviating impact of economic growth. "Poverty rates would have been lower had the economies in question been able to achieve the growth in mean per capita expenditure that they did but with their previous and more equal distributions."

Which brings me to the proverbial million dollar question—Is it even possible for these two to go hand in hand? Is economic growth that is driven by free markets and loose regulation, as is the one that has been embraced by many Asian countries over the last two decades, compatible with an egalitarian society? Or is such a growth the very agent that kindles inequality in the first place?

A cursory analysis seems to support the latter proposition. A capitalist economy rewards—with income being the reward—initiative, skill, education, labor, and capital. The fewer of these you possess, the less is the eventual reward you walk away with. Empirical data further reinforces this sometimes anecdotally perceived causality. As shown in Figure A.3, income inequality started rising after a brief drop a few years into the launch of the Chinese economic reform in the late 1970s and hasn't looked back since. Likewise, inequality in India also began

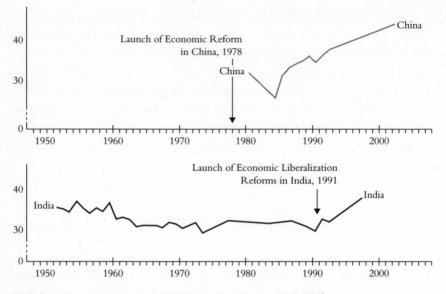

Figure A.3   Tracking the Gini Index for China and India[15]

its consistently upward climb only after the liberalization reforms were launched in 1991.

It is not my intention however to prosecute economic liberalism for the ills of inequality. To do so would be to close one's eyes to the body of evidence that indicates otherwise. A comprehensive study published in 2007 by the Economic Freedom Network testified that there is nothing inherent in the idea of a free economy that worsens the state of its poor.[16] On the contrary, the authors of the report found that the freer a country is economically, the higher the income of its poorest, together with a better average income, life expectancy, and environment.

The real agents of inequality lie not in free-market driven growth itself, but one level below, in how this growth has traditionally been unevenly distributed across geographical regions (urban vs. rural) and industry sectors (nonagricultural vs. agricultural).[17]

And herein lies the understanding that guides us to the answer to Asia's biggest challenge today. Income redistribution or social redress measures as solutions are incomplete, ineffective or worse because they often follow from a case of mistaken provenance of economic inequality. Numbers that demonstrate a worsening inequality aren't so much a disease that needs a cure, but more a symptom indicative of the real malaise—that unevenly distributed economic growth offers uneven opportunities across peoples, translating into unevenly distributed income and hence economic inequality.

In the long run, it is opportunity and not income that we should strive to equalize. It will not eradicate inequality. But it will be an important step towards preventing it from growing further without compromising continued economic growth.

The ESLH Framework

What remains then is for us to translate this idea of equality of opportunity into a set of policy guidelines. A detailed prescription of such recommendations is out of scope for this essay. Instead, what I would like to do is to outline a framework (let's call it the Economic Sustainability Lessons from History, or ESLH, framework) that can allow us to use empirical macroeconomic data from global economic history to pick out these guidelines ourselves.

Keeping in mind that any recipe for more equality that compromises on economic growth is unlikely to be palatable to policy makers, investors or economists, the underlying idea of the ESLH Framework is to hunt for instances in the history of developing nations where income inequality has fallen even as the economy has continued to grow. Once

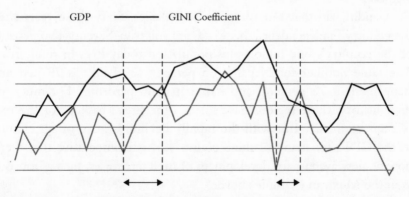

Figure A.4   The ESLH Framework Relates to Periods in Economic History (Shown by Arrows) When Rising GDP Accompanies a Falling Gini Index[18]

identified, these windows of economic history can then be studied further for specific policies that were designed to equalize opportunities and correspondingly succeeded in equalizing incomes, while maintaining economic growth.

To see this framework in action, we can look at the example of Mexico (see Figure A.4). Between 1999 and 2008, Mexico's Gini coefficient fell 7 percentage points from 53 to 46, less than any recorded score for the country in the last 60 years.[19] In the same period, the country's real GDP continued to grow at an average rate of around 3 percent.[20]

What counsel can we draw from this experience? No doubt, the economies of Latin America and Asia are different, and there are things that worked in Mexico's favor that aren't applicable to Asia. But surely there should be a few ingredients of Mexico's success that can offer Asia a lesson in balancing economic growth with equality of opportunity.

There is at least one: the country's focus on rural development. A depreciation in rural poverty contributed significantly to Mexico's economic growth as well as its tempering inequality over the last decade. "Between 2000 and 2004, extreme poverty fell almost 7 percentage points, which can be explained by development in rural areas, where extreme poverty fell from 42.4 percent to 27.9 percent."[21]

According to the World Bank, the factors that contributed to this reduction include "macroeconomic stability . . . and the diversification of income from nonagricultural activities, such as tourism and services"— arguably also applicable in equal measure in at least some parts of emerging Asia.

Gandhi said that India lives in her villages. Sixty-three years after the country's independence, his words are still true. Seventy-two percent of the country's one-billion-plus population today lives in rural areas. The same number for Nepal is 85 percent, Sri Lanka is 79 percent, Bangladesh is 76 percent, and Pakistan is 66 percent.[22] For much of their history, these regions have formed the bread baskets for the rest of their countries. But with the rapidly declining share of agriculture in the GDPs for many of these countries,[23] it is imperative that there now be new avenues for development of rural territories, such as tourism as in the Mexican example above.

Bringing growth to the country-side, instead of luring village folk the other way with the glitter of swanky metropolitan development offers many advantages. It opens up new opportunities for the inhabitants of those areas without requiring them to desert their families or familiar landscapes. It reduces migratory pressures on urban centres, many of which in Asia are reeling from the effects of an exploding population density and an overburdened infrastructure. And it attracts more investment to the rural areas, allowing for economic growth to continue and at the same time be spread more evenly across communities.

Eliciting from the Mexican experience then, we have at least one strategic guideline that Asian leaders can follow in pursuing the goal of Inclusive Development: emphasis on rural development. There is of course no reason to stop at one. Following the ESLH Framework can allow for other such lessons to be learnt from economic histories of other countries as well that may be applicable in this region.

Conclusion

In many circles in emerging Asia, the recent financial crisis is already being talked about as history. A history that will teach us some lessons, but will not repeat itself, not in the immediate future at least. The future is bright. In the relentless journey of Asia's economic bandwagon however, a growing number of its poor are being thrown off the cart along the way. Rising economic inequality now plagues countries across the continent's expanse, and threatens to undermine the very purpose that the polity of the region swears by: economic growth for its people.

It is essential for the long-term sustainability of this growth that Asian countries pursue a model of Inclusive Development, that offers a stake in the fruits of this progress to their poorest. The ESLH framework outlined in this essay helps us discover periods in our economic history when economic growth did not come at the expense of rising economic inequality, and learn from them. Nevertheless, this framework is but one step towards formulating an effective response. The key point is this—unless we are able to ensure that economic development creates new opportunities for each and every one amongst us, we may just be laying the stage for more men and women to give up hopes for a better future and resort to the business of selling paper tissues on street sidewalks.

Notes

1. "U.S. economy back on track; IMF raises Asia forecast." Dated: October 29, 2009.

2. "Analysis: IMF challenges Asia to change its economic habits." Dated: July 19, 2010.

3. "'More poor' in India than Africa." Dated: July 13, 2010.

4. CIA—The World Factbook. South Asia—India.

5. "Study estimates China's rich hiding $1.4 trillion." Dated: August 13, 2010.

6. "Inequality in Asia, Key Indicators 2007, Highlights." Report by Asian Development Bank.

7. Ibid.

8. This chart is taken from page 6 of "Inequality in Asia, Key indicators 2007, Highlights." Report by Asian Development Bank.

9. This claim is taken from the Wikipedia page for "Economic Inequality," which labels it as having been referenced from Wilkinson, Richard; Pickett, Kate (2009). *The Spirit Level: Why More Equal Societies Almost Always Do Better.* Allen Lane. pp. 352. ISBN 1846140396.

10. "Some Got Rich First—and Richer Later." Dated: May 2010.

11. "UN report reveals deep social divide in Thailand." Dated: June 23, 2010.

12. This data was taken from the Wikipedia entry for "Kuznets curve," where it is marked as having been referenced from "the sources presented by Alice Hansen Jones (1775); Edward Wolff (1915–1995)."

13. "Some Got Rich First—and Richer Later." Dated: May 2010.

14. This figure is taken from the Wikipedia entry for "Kuznets curve," where it is marked as being a "Hypothetical Kuznets curve. Empirically observed curves aren't smooth or symmetrical." The caption of the figure also includes a reference to the article "The Richer-Is-Greener Curve" for examples of "real" curves.

15. This figure was referenced from the chart "Gini Index—Income Disparity since World War II" on the Wikipedia entry for "Gini coefficient." The chart is an original work authored by user Cflm001 "from publicly available data from the World Bank, Nationmaster, and the U.S. Census Bureau."

16. Chapter 1: "Economic Freedom of the World," 2007. Economic Freedom of the World: 2009 Annual Report.

17. "Inequality in Asia, Key Indicators 2007, Highlights." Report by Asian Development Bank.

18. This figure was referenced from the chart "Gini Index—Income Disparity since World War II" on the Wikipedia entry for "Gini coefficient." The

chart is an original work authored by user Cflm001 "from publicly available data from the World Bank, Nationmaster, and the U.S. Census Bureau."

19. This data was taken from the chart "Gini Index—Income Disparity since World War II" on the Wikipedia entry for "Gini coefficient." The chart is an original work authored by user Cflm001 "from publicly available data from the World Bank, Nationmaster, and the U.S. Census Bureau."

20. This data was taken from the chart "Average annual GDP growth by period" on the Wikipedia entry for "Economy of Mexico," where it is marked as having been collected from a set of three sources: i. Crandall, R (September 30, 2004). "Mexico's Domestic Economy," in Crandall, R; Paz, G; Roett, R. Mexico's Democracy at Work: Political and Economic Dynamics. Lynne Reiner Publishers. ISBN 10-1588263002; ii. Cruz Vasconcelos, Gerardo. "Desempeño Histórico 1914–2004" (PDF). Retrieved February 17, 2007; and iii. "IMF World Economic Outlook Database, April 2010." Retrieved July 24, 2010.

21. "Mexico: Income Generation and Social Protection for the Poor." Dated: August 24, 2005.

22. Nationmaster People Statistics > Percentage living in rural areas. (most recent) by country.

23. "Rapid growth of selected Asian economies. Lessons and implications for agriculture and food security: Synthesis report." FAO Regional Office for Asia and the Pacific. Dated: April 2006.

Healthcare in Asia: A Roadmap for the Next Decade

By Gemlyn George

It was the winter of 1777. Soldiers of the newly formed continental army under George Washington had encamped at Valley Forge. Over the next four months, typhoid, dysentery, and small pox swept through the camp decimating an already weak force. Washington and his medics decided to act on a rumor that small pox could be prevented. They decided to rub the pus of already affected individuals into wounds of unaffected men. Of the men inoculated, only a small number went on to develop the disease but the rest were rendered immune for life. This along with measures to improve sanitation with a dedicated corps of doctors and nurses helped the army recover and reengage the British with new confidence, eventually winning independence.

History is replete with such instances where health was often the decisive factor in shaping events. In the turmoil following World War II, when Asian nations took the form they have now, healthcare was acknowledged as an important factor in the road to prosperity.

In the year 2000, the World Health Organization (WHO) conducted its first-ever analysis of the health systems of 191 member states. The top 50 included 12 countries from Asia. But a disproportionate number among those—nine—belonged to oil producing nations. The subsequent decade played host to numerous stories of Asian nations coming into their own with robustly growing economies weathering the global economic storm, and yet there has a been a sense of disquiet when it comes to healthcare. Despite noises made at the beginning of the millennium, expenditure in this sector by governments across the region has often been seconded in preference to measures that reaped quick rewards, such as physical infrastructure and arms, in terms of economic growth and a greater diplomatic punch. As a result, Asian countries continue to lag behind in healthcare as can be seen by the dreadfully high numbers in infant mortality in South Asia—52 per thousand in India alone.

Another worrying trend is the paucity of healthcare professionals. India has approximately 70,000 doctors, working out to 7 per 10,000 people, and 1.5 million nurses and technicians for her 1.2 billion strong population (WHO data). Compare this with countries with strong healthcare satisfaction levels which average above 25 doctors per 10,000. Within the WHO list, Singapore was the highest ranked Asian country at 6, while Myanmar brought up the rear at 190. China came in at 144 and India was placed at 112. Contrast this with the size of their economies. China is the second largest economy in the world and India the fourth largest. Yet, the investment made in this sector has a lot of catching up to do.

Why Is It So Important for Healthcare to Refine Its Act?

In 2003, a paper by David Bloom and his team highlighted that one year's improvement in a population's life expectancy could result in a 4 percent increase in output. Illness and disability reduce hourly wages earned, an effect especially seen in developing countries. It's imperative therefore that a nation looking to move forward also allocates resources to ensure that her people can function at their best. Interestingly, the success of the existing system in reducing mortality due to infectious diseases with a changing lifestyle means that Asian people have a greater life expectancy and in turn have begun to face a new spectrum of chronic disorders.

To illustrate the changing spectrum of healthcare needs using China as a model, currently 6 percent of her population is diabetic, 20 percent hypertensive, and 25 percent overweight. Topping this, 30 percent of the population continue to smoke (WHO). A population cohort with the above problems will require several multi-disciplinarian visits over the next 20 years, dealing with the problem in itself and other clinical offshoots. For example, being a diabetic increases a person's risk for cardiac and renal disease over a period of time, thus placing a strain on other branches of the health system. Combine this need for chronic care with a vastly undermanned system and things do not look too good. South Asia also offers similar challenges, with chronic diseases a priority in urban centers while infectious diseases remain a scourge and the main killer in the rural hinterland.

Confounding the obvious state of under-preparedness the sector faces, is the financial model countries in the region employ to pay for healthcare. The Middle Eastern countries employ a mix of public (funded by petrodollars, heavily subsidized) and private sector hospitals (paid for by insurance or direct fees) to take care of their health systems. Other nations like Singapore [and] South Korea mandate universal insurance [coverage] for everyone, paid for by varying degrees by the individual, the employer, and the rest subsidized by the government (40 to 60 percent depending on country). The government also has healthcare safety nets for those who cannot afford insurance.

Looking at South Asia and India in particular, the scenario suddenly turns very bleak. India currently spends 4 percent of her GDP on healthcare of which government spending accounts for a measly 19 percent. Compare this to France where 11 percent of her GDP is on healthcare, of which government spending is 79 percent (World Bank data). France of course has the highest satisfaction rates for her health system. In some areas of India, especially the rural sector, health spending can form a disproportionate figure of up to 18 percent of income. In addition there is a huge manpower crisis in the existing network of primary care facilities with a 15.1 percent shortfall in doctors and up to 56.8 percent in multi-health workers (Bulletin on Rural Health Statistics 2008). This of course is not including the large rates of absenteeism and the already existing shortfall in the required number of primary health centers.

China to start with had an excellent network of rural practitioners (barefoot doctors) and a centralized healthcare system which made tremendous gains in life expectancy, by a series of public health measures including sanitation, immunization, and control of disease vectors. With Deng Xiaoping's revolution in the early 1980s, the apparently successful model of health was dismantled overnight without an adequate replacement. This happened through a reduction in funding from the central government for hospitals, in which the onus was placed on the province. There was also a change in pricing policy which enabled hospitals to make huge profits on new procedures and drugs. The commune system which had served most of rural China was also dismantled overnight and the public health system was decentralized and partially privatized (Blumenthal NEJM 2005).

All this contributed to creating a system that was ranked 188 among 191 nations by the WHO in the year 2000. Subsequently, however, massive government spending ($125 billion from 2009 to 2011) promises to alleviate the situation with an aim to cover 90 percent of the population with insurance by 2011 and universal healthcare by 2020. This of course does not address the basic problem of high drug costs and lack of accessibility of quality care for all.

Therein lies the next problem. An increasingly affluent population has come to expect the same level of service in healthcare as they would in other sectors. The inadequacy of the system to match up to expectations of service levels and an unrealistic expectation of a quick cure leads to great levels of dissatisfaction. Match this with a belief (true in many cases) that doctors indulge in a system where expensive investigations and drugs help line their pockets through a "cut" system and suddenly the sector seems to be in turmoil. Recent reports of increasing levels of violence against healthcare workers in China and India illustrates this problem.

To summarize, the two big engines of economic growth in Asia (South Asia and China) have healthcare systems that are fragmented, suffer huge deficits of manpower and facilities, and are potential flashpoints of anger to a young population that is increasingly demanding the best possible care. Further complicating the scenario is the presence of traditional systems of medicine, which often operate in unregulated areas without proper checks and controls.

This brings us back to the root question: why didn't anyone think about this ten years ago? Simple: quick returns. Build a road or an airport, investment flows into the region and in a few years, the whole region gets transformed. Healthcare however, with its long training periods (6–12 years for a doctor and 4–8 years for allied professionals), takes a much longer period to show any tangible benefits, often up to a generation.

What's the Solution?

The most successful and effective healthcare systems around the world like Cuba, France, and Japan place strong emphasis on community based healthcare programs. Effective care at the community level and a well stratified system of referral means resources get allocated to people who need it the most and at the same time ensures that high-tech healthcare can still be practiced. To illustrate this with an example, a person suffering from acute diarrhea does not need to consult a gastroenterologist with 12 years of medical school behind him to get a simple course of antibiotics.

This is exactly what post-revolution China pursued so effectively and India tried to implement after its independence. Subsequently, though, in one case the system was dismantled without an effective alternative in place, and in the other, there just wasn't enough investment in manpower and resources. Other nations in Asia all have systems based on the above model and work quite well within the constraints of resources.

Just like any system, healthcare too depends on the triumvirate of manpower, infrastructure, and finance. Governments across Asia have recognized this and have allocated resources or planned to do so. Nations like Singapore and South Korea have invested heavily, looking to transform themselves to the forefront of medical research and healthcare (indirectly attracting medical tourism dollars). Of the South Asian nations, India has been mulling over the creation of a new cadre of health workers to support and serve the rural areas in addition to the creation of multiple institutions dedicated to super specialty care and cutting edge research.

All these reforms would be pointless if the common man for whom all this is meant, can't access or pay for it. Once again, governments have been proactive in this area. Most Asian countries have an existing network of insurance or fee based healthcare and only have to ramp it up. China has spent $120 billion in the last 3 years to try and achieve 90 percent coverage of its citizens. In India, several states have launched insurance schemes and the central government bankrolls 75 percent of the National Health Insurance Scheme which aims to help households living below the poverty line with liabilities arising from hospitalization. For a nation that has only 15 percent of its population insured, this scheme has helped cover 55 million people or another 5 percent gain access to healthcare. But most importantly for India, it is the poorest of the poor that get covered.

The only "catch" with all this action is that it is designed to bring the existing health system to levels that would have been acceptable or excellent at the turn of the century. What it does not do is create the framework needed to help push the frontier of medicine, cement Asia's place at the forefront of new development and at the same time provide effective, quality healthcare to the man on the street. To draw a corollary, healthcare today, as a system, is where computing was 30 years ago, a series of stand-alone mainframes which one went to in order to get a process done. What we need in health is a paradigm similar to the IT world today. A world where a search result is tailored based on past search patterns. A networked, integrated world where processes are fine tuned to deliver maximum efficiency.

I believe that while governments are ramping up infrastructure projects to meet demand, it makes sense to also create a backbone of IT enabled services and use it to enhance the experience of the "art of medicine." Around the globe and in almost every other field, IT is used to integrate systems and connect people. An executive sitting in an office can track events at a plant on the other side of the globe. The health system unfortunately has nothing similar at the moment as it operates as a standalone system. Patient records are kept in an office; if the patient decides to switch doctors, all that is provided is a summary of the previous hospitalization. In the process, vital and potentially life-saving information is often missed.

Imagine a system that is digitized. Patient data is collected, stored into a centralized server. If he should go to another doctor, the other provider will still be able to access previous heath history from the cloud servers. This way, healthcare providers also get a clearer picture of the disease process, information does not get missed, duplicity in investigations gets avoided, potentially increasing efficiency and thus delivering cost savings. The patient could be identified with a unique ID number (similar to the UID project in India) with a smart card, which [would] carry details about insurance providers, blood group, and organ donor details. The possibilities are limitless.

In any field, measurement of data is the single most important method to see if a process is working. Any company will be able to give a person real-time data of how they are performing. Take a car company. Quarterly, sometimes monthly, sales reports, profit reports, etc. can be provided. Healthcare however takes an enormous time to measure the few numbers that it does (e.g., infant mortality rate). Providing data on number of patients visited or surgeries done, etc. is never really done due to the sheer absence of a system to measure data. Being able to measure data could potentially influence policy decisions tremendously.

What is more important, however, is the kind of opportunities this could open up for public health. Take clinical trials for example. Having a centralized system recording clinical events eliminates the need for teams of people following patients and collecting data. All it requires is a person with a computer at the other end evaluating data. What's more, this also means data gets disseminated faster. That is, the time from introduction into a trial to actual use gets reduced tremendously due to the time savings involved. In addition, this provides healthcare workers with a network that allows them access to the latest in evidence-based medicine; flags that go up for potential adverse effects with drugs helps enhance patient care and decreases the number of iatrogenic events that could happen.

Just to illustrate how having greater connectivity could transform the way medicine is practiced, take the field of microbiology. Antibiotic resistance suddenly seems to be on everyone's radar. With increasing medical tourism, the possibility of super-bugs crossing continents and flourishing elsewhere suddenly seems a very real possibility. Antibiotic resistance occurs due to indiscriminate and inadequate use of existing drugs. Having a central system allows information about community-based susceptibility tests to be disseminated to all practitioners. Physicians prescribe only what is recommended and follow the protocol strictly. Reports of drug resistance are followed up immediately by the national equivalent of the Centers for Disease Control (CDC) and quarantined.

Even in the case of emerging viral illnesses (e.g., SARS or H1N1), the only tool we have is the speed with which index cases are identified. In this age of just-in-time logistics, does it make sense to hang on to antiquated methods of reporting? Can we really afford the delay in recognizing the emergence of new pathogens? The only way is to act faster and the best way to make sure that happens is by having an effective reporting system.

Applying the same principle of data mining could potentially revolutionize fields like genetics which need a huge database of people to be screened before an association between a gene and a disease can be made. As we begin to understand the increasing complexity with which our environment influences all aspects of our health from our genes to the way we age, having a comprehensive database will be an enormous resource in picking out potential cause and effect relationships in addition to highlighting new areas of research. The embryonic field of environmental medicine would gain an enormous fillip.

Traditional systems of medicine in Asia have always stressed the impact of our surroundings on us. The systems as we know today are riddled with several problems. For one there is no authority overseeing and enforcing a minimum standard of care. Second, traditional medicines often have high levels of heavy metals. Creating a local equivalent of the Food and Drug Administration (FDA) dedicated to ensuring the drugs used adhere to strict manufacturing standards and regular toxicity screening would increase transparency in this sector. Third, integration of the system along with allopathic medicine in the above proposed IT speedway. This would ensure accountability and unlock potential applications in research.

Effective medical care today requires a multi-disciplinarian approach. Having a multi-tiered system of referral ultimately provides the best results. In the future however, with the emergence of a rapidly aging population, geriatrics and hospice care will undoubtedly gain prominence. Integration of these disciplines into grass roots primary healthcare will become essential to help people live their lives with dignity. To sum up, sustainable prosperity is virtually impossible without a strong health system taking care of every citizen's needs. The healthcare system in Asia (barring some countries) is one of massive disparity, gross understaffing, underfunding, corruption, and creaking inefficiency. The good news is, with Asia's new found economic might, an overhaul of this sector is very plausible. A process, which in itself will provide the impetus for growth in our economies, will propel and cement us in our rightful place as the center of the world.

Asia's Challenge 2020: Getting the Basics Right

By Rohit Pathak

As Asia marches forward, as some of its nations join the industrial world, and as others, although still young, establish themselves among the globe's economic and political elite, the world watches in bewildering awe the continent which it once had tagged as the Third World. There is no doubt, therefore, that the coming decade will be Asia's. In fact, it might not be an exaggeration to say that this entire century will be Asia's. But amidst all this glory, as is the case with every transition, there are certain obstacles that can severely stymie the continent's progress and must be removed before anything more complex is to be achieved. I am, of course, talking about those problems that the developing part of Asia is still dealing with.

Quite surprisingly, while some nations such as Japan, Singapore, and South Korea have been successful in ascending to First World resplendency, there still are nations in the continent that are struggling with dithering political regimes, rampant corruption, poverty, hunger and malnutrition, poor healthcare, illiteracy, and internal instabilities—all the characteristics that are unacceptable if the goal is comprehensive development. There are yet others (such as India) which, despite robust economic growth, stable governments and noble government intentions, still remain unsuccessful in providing basic sustenance to a large part of their population, again perhaps because of the transitory corruption that has permeated the system. Then there is also the issue of energy security in a ruthlessly energy-hungry, oil-devouring economic environment under the threat of an imminent energy crisis and amidst increasing pressure from nature and the international community to go green.

The challenges, as we can see, are many, and therefore, in my view, to think of the problems in terms of a "one greatest challenge" is to disregard the other equally significant challenges as unimportant. It is also futile to target them one at a time just for the sake of correcting unpleasant statistics, as these problems are, and have invariably been, inherently interconnected. And so, what we need as a continent are not small and superficial remedies but a single holistic solution that incorporates all aspects of all our problems. However romantically promising, a holistic solution still eludes our policy makers, perhaps because it is too theoretical and idealistic. To make things easier for our continent's leaders, it is, then, only wise to break down these problems to the most fundamental and come up with the "most" holistic solution.

Upon doing so, I believe the basic problem that hinders most of our progress (especially economic) is still the problem of governance. Without good governance, all policies, plans or solutions are redundant. The biggest hurdle in the way of good governance is corruption, as it is, undoubtedly, the direct and indirect cause of almost the entire spectrum of our problems such as poverty, terrorism, illiteracy, poor infrastructure and others, which probably, in its absence, could have been solved by now. On the domestic level, therefore, besides increasing the efficiency of our countries' government machinery, our primary aim must be to develop an effective framework for tackling the govern-mental menace of corruption. Furthermore, on a bigger and broader scale and in view of a more general and long-term picture of Asia, our leaders must also make efforts to produce a peaceful political envi-ronment in Asia by attaining greater political stability in tense regions such as Myanmar, Afghanistan, Pakistan, and the Middle East so as to make these regions economically stable and reliable and capable of a more active participation in our economic environment. Without it, nothing greater can be expected of them and the economic potential of regional integration and cooperation cannot be fully realized. Not only that, we will need all the help we can get from these nations in tackling the harsher challenges that await us.

I admit that in the midst of immensely pressing issues like global warming, energy security, and sustainable development, what I have proposed is a rather dry diagnosis, but alas, as with every task, I believe it is the dull part that ought to be dealt with first, especially in Asia where it can prove to be a huge hindrance in the future. The premise is as simple as it can get: if the foundation is solid, the building will stand.

Consider this story recently featured in an article in the *New York Times* of an illiterate and poor farmer, Ratan Bhuria, with a malnourished wife and children in the village of Jhabua, Madhya Pradesh, India. Under a Union Government policy for ensuring nutrition and food security to the poor, as a person below the poverty line, he and his family are entitled monthly to a 77-pound bag of grains, sugar and kerosene. Unfortunately, no matter how much money is allotted to the scheme, they don't receive it. The article also states "Studies show that 70 percent of a roughly $12 billion budget is wasted, stolen or absorbed by bureaucratic and transportation costs." On top of that, the local clerks who are supposed to issue food rations to families such as Mr. Bhuria's seldom do their job. In an instance, investigators once, as the report states "discovered 3,500 fake food ration booklets in the district, believed to have been issued by low-level officials for themselves and their friends." The Union Government of India, with its noble intentions of ensuring food security to every citizen below the poverty line, has a reasonably good policy in place, has considerable funding for the project, and even has a widespread Public Distribution System (PDS) along with an army of bureaucratic workforce in villages to ensure the distribution of food grains at the lowest level—all in vain, unfortunately, because of the unredeemed presence of corruption. To see all efforts evaporate just because of selfish inefficiencies of a few is nauseatingly frustrating and detestable.

Corruption is an economic parasite that debilitates all functioning aspects of a socio-economic system. Nepotism, by reducing competitiveness, severely undermines the principles of a capitalist economic system and destroys the fabric of a democratic government system. So it is not wrong to say that a corrupt democracy is as good as a despotic feudal monarchy. On the macroeconomic scale, by significantly increasing public expenditure on the one hand and by reducing the tax take on the other, bribery, along with other corrupt practices, significantly raises the costs of operating an economy, which eventually leads to financial damage in the form of fiscal deficits and macroeconomic instability. This fact was unequivocally highlighted in the event of the near collapse of the highly corrupt economies of Thailand, Korea, and Indonesia in 1997 during the East Asian financial crisis. The Philippines, which was once ahead of the South Asian nations such as India in the 1950s in economic terms, also trails behind some of them today, only because of its internal corruption. Furthermore, on a more social and humanitarian level, apart from corroding the legitimacy and the trust of the state, corruption usually hurts the poor as it ruthlessly and shamelessly sucks out most of the already bare essentials that they sustain themselves on. As Mr. Bhuria's example demonstrates, it is one of the single biggest obstacles in the way of eliminating poverty. And in Asia, where most of the countries are still at the developing stages, because it eats away the hard earned resources required for development, corruption, according to me, is absolutely unacceptable.

Upon observing closely the 2009 statistics of Transparency International's Corruption Perceptions Index (CPI), it also does not come as a surprise that the most corrupt nations of Asia are the least developed and the most unstable. According to CPI's 2009 statistics, Afghanistan, Myanmar, and Iraq—all politically turbulent nations—scored 1.3, 1.4, and 1.5 whereas Singapore, Hong Kong, and Japan scored 9.2, 8.2, and 7.7 respectively, strictly in accordance with the perceived relationship. What concerns me is that most of the nations in Asia, especially those of South and Southeast Asia, including prosperous ones such as India, scored below 5 in the CPI. This indicates an even greater need for our continent's leaders to eradicate this pestering menace.

Although various anti-corruption efforts have [gained] momentum in the past decade (such as the G-20's commitment towards the ratification and implementation of the UN Convention Against Corruption) not much has been achieved, especially in informing the inaccessible poor and the illiterate—the most in need of this information. Apart from strong political will and an efficient judiciary that would strictly ensure law enforcement, extricating the people from the shackles of a corrupt government requires transparency (in the form of better availability of information) and accountability in the government, along with an active civil society and a free media. Such solutions are well known. The fundamental problem, however, is that corruption is a problem beyond politics and despite the presence of extensive and vigorous anti-corruption laws and policies, the implementation and execution invariably depends on the prevalent government, which can show either nature, depending on the luck of that country. Thus, although this implementation does require, on part of the public office, some degree of patriotism, honesty, and selflessness, the hope that such abstract qualities will eventually permeate the bearers of public office cannot be relied upon in the formulation of a scientific economic policy where predictability is often synonymous with certainty and accuracy. This, therefore, calls for the removal of control of the human element from the government machinery and thereby, ironically, increasing trust by another fairer and more precise method. Utilizing the powers of Information Technology, then, becomes almost inevitable.

In this regard, the views of David Cameron, the British prime minister, are particularly interesting. In one of his talks, Mr. Cameron described how the availability of information can dilute the centralized state structure and can take us to a "post-bureaucratic age" where, by giving more power and control to the people and by "marrying" this fact with the incredible abundance of information, we can "remake politics, remake government, and remake our public services." He gives an example of how greater transparency can be achieved through this unique marriage of governance with IT through "one of his favorite websites"—the Missouri Accountability Portal. It seems only wise to quote him verbatim: "In the old days, only the government could hold the information. . . . Now here, on one website, one state in America, every single dollar spent by that government is searchable, is analyzable, is checkable." It is amply clear that only through such transparency and accountability on the part of the government can we eliminate corruption from our system.

The wonders of IT can help us do exactly that in preventing or at least reducing corruption in the first place and at the lowest level where it matters most. Let's come back to the example of Mr. Bhuria. Because of the patent failures of the PDS, the Indian Government is already contemplating scrapping the distribution system altogether and is planning to directly give food coupons or cash to families below the poverty line so as to save them the trouble of facing corrupt PDS staff and bureaucrats by giving them the freedom to buy whatever things they wish and from wherever they wish. Such a move is welcome, and it gives policy makers enough ground to speculate and plan further. Thus, for instance, to ensure the delivery of these food coupons to families such as those of Mr. Bhuria, these coupons could be made electronic (say, like a credit card) and could be designed to contain, along with other essential identification information, accurate biometric details of every person in the family, associating them with the already proposed Unique Identification Number—an ID number along the lines of the Social Security number in the United States. A network of retail stores could then be set up in remote rural areas by private players, replacing the government PDS. Minimizing government-individual interference, the system would require an entitled person to purchase directly from the private retailer in exchange for his coupon, the coupons being allowed, of course, for later reimbursement. The precise biometric data, along with verification at the time of purchase, would also ascertain that the supplies actually go to the families themselves. This would keep in check the issuing of fake coupons.

Finally, to ensure that big retailers actually set up shops in remote rural areas, the companies could be advised to include this undertaking as a part of their corporate social responsibility. Printing an indicator on the company's products and other advertisings that would project the company's efforts in this area could also be made mandatory for the purpose of reflecting these initiatives in that company's marketing, thereby incentivizing them to open such shops in exchange for a better market image. Additionally, if this entire consumer-supplier transaction data of the central database is made visible or accessible to the public, then policy experts could also pick up critical patterns that could help them improve upon their existing schemes. So basically, with the help of information technology, we can create a transparent and accountable system that will "accurately" deliver. Similarly, in other areas of governance, the transparency produced by IT can be used in substantially reducing corruption. It is, admittedly, radical, but it's still worth a try.

So, in sum, we could say that a healthy government structure is a prerequisite for all other forms of social and economic development. Therefore, just as important as eradicating corruption in the domestic context is also achieving political stability in the larger, much broader, context of the continent. It is worth recalling here what the Minister Mentor of Singapore, Lee Kuan Yew said about the rising instability in Myanmar: "ASEAN leaders know that if the situation in Myanmar deteriorates and continues to deteriorate, there will come a breaking point where much more brutal force will be used to put a revolt down. . . . So it is in the best interests of every country in ASEAN to help stabilize Myanmar. An unstable Myanmar is a time bomb for the whole region." Indeed, political instability in a country, besides threatening the general security of the surrounding region, cripples growth in not only that country but also the entire neighborhood. For the nation in particular, the uncertainty associated with an unstable political environment, in addition to detrimentally impacting executive economic decisions such as investment, production, and labor supply, reduces foreign and domestic investment and hence the speed of economic development. And, most importantly, the hostile presence of such unstable countries disrupts cooperation between bordering countries, severely undermining the otherwise great economic potential of that area.

Therefore, instability in any region will be detrimental to the entire continent in the future. A stable political region, on the other hand, by providing an atmosphere conducive to regional economic integration and cooperation, will immensely benefit the economic prosperity of different neighborhoods, which will consequently contribute to the overall prosperity of Asia. For example, if the struggling countries in South Asia resolve their conflicts and gain more stability and if trade restrictions are removed, it is expected that intra-regional trade, which is presently at $5 billion, could jump to $20 billion. Moreover, a peaceful region, especially in and around Afghanistan and the Middle-East, would also solve to a great extent the festering problem of international terrorism. Thus, Asian leaders must make efforts towards brokering peace between belligerent nations to enhance stability in tense regions. Also, for the purpose of manufacturing a harmonious inter-country cooperative economic environment, Asian leaders must make efforts towards enhancing market integration and cooperation as part of their regional strategy. In this regard, organizations such as ASEAN and SAARC, some of which haven't yet delivered successfully, must deliver. Unfortunately, it is true that regional conflicts and instability will prevail for a long time. Nonetheless, as responsible nations of Asia, mature economies must make all possible efforts in assisting their ailing counterparts in coming out of political misery, perhaps through conditional aid and, if necessary, even (peaceful) intervention.

It is also important to mention here that democracy, too, is a vital part of the definition of a "healthy government structure" majorly because, besides giving the people adequate rights and freedom, it plays an essential role in "sustainable" stability and growth. Although upon observing, it does seem that certain oppressive authoritative regimes such as the highly corrupt military junta of Myanmar, the Kim Jong-Il-led nuclear armed totalitarian government of North Korea, and quite surprisingly, also China, by maintaining a long presence, have stabilized their internal politics, this apparent stability is actually a state of unstable equilibrium where there is a constant possibility of a revolt or an uprising. Spreading the light of democracy in regions with such closed and oppressive governments by encouraging them to resort to more democratic practices will ensure sustainable peace along with sustainability in all other aspects of growth, and so diligent efforts must be made in this direction as well.

This chapter in Asia's history will be all about economic development. We have all the pieces necessary to solve the economic puzzle except those that complete the picture of good governance in the region. On finding those pieces and upon completing this part of the puzzle, economic growth will be smarter, accelerated, more inclusive, more sustainable, and capable of confronting the long unresolved problems of poverty, food security, illiteracy and even terrorism and energy security. It is time, therefore, that we got our basics right for, in the decade after the next and the ones after that, we will have even grimmer challenges to face, and we better be prepared for them.

References

www.nytimes.com/2010/08/09/world/asia/09food.html?_r=1&scp=3&sq=india%20poverty&st=cse.

Vinay_Bhargava, Emil_Bolongaita-Challenging_Corruption_in_Asia.

www.philippinecorruption.net/.

http://wiki.galbijim.com/Asian_financial_crisis.

www.transparency.org/policy_research/surveys_indices/cpi/2009/cpi_2009_table.

www.ted.com/talks/david_cameron.html.

www.transparency.org/news_room/latest_news/press_releases/2009/2009_11_17_cpi2009_en.

http://dassk.org/index.php?topic=6304.0.

Sadiq_Ahmed, Saman_Kelegama, Ejaz_Ghani- Promoting_Economic_Cooperation_ in_South_Asia: Beyond_SAFTA.

www.ssc.upenn.edu/ier/Political%20Economy%20Archives/Political%20Econo my%20Working%20Papers/Political%20Instability.pdf.

Decoupling from the West

By Loh Su Hsing

Strong growth in recent decades and the relatively quick recovery of Asia from the financial crisis has sparked debates on whether Asia is decoupling from the West. But perhaps what is more pertinent is the normative question of *whether Asia should* decouple from the West and exactly what this decoupling process entails.

Loosely interpreted, decoupling is said to happen when two entities move in opposite directions, disconnect, or [one] no longer has a direct effect on the other. This essay argues that Asia should decouple from the West, and that this process of decoupling will be the greatest challenge that Asia will face in the coming decade. However, a more measured definition of decoupling is used—the overarching process whereby Asia *explores, diversifies, and reduces general reliance on the West.* The key is to engage and cooperate with the West but allow more room for Asia to find its own niche and maximize its potential. It is not a zero-sum game and it is certainly not about disengaging from the West or isolating Asia.

It might seem misguided to focus on the macro issue of decoupling when there are many other specific challenges plaguing Asia, spanning from environmental problems to instability in domestic politics. However, closer examination would reveal that decoupling is an overarching process that underlies practically all of these realms. Due to the eminence of the West in the recent centuries, its norms, values, standards and methods have become the de facto hardware and software of the world, and Asia is often at the receiving end. Continued reliance and benchmarking against the West in all these realms is not the way forward. Much has been written about finding the "Asian Way," but this is very much a misnomer and the concept remains nebulous. Truth of the matter is, nothing in this globalized and interdependent world is completely unique these days, and what we have are merely adaptations and improvements. What is suggested here is not a singularly

173

Asian or "un-Western" way, but rather adaptations, improvements, and leapfrogging from what is already in existence.

Sketching Asia

Several qualifiers are necessary at this juncture. The usage of "Asia" and the "West" is not always meaningful, and suggests rather erroneously that the two are opposites, and each are coherent, homogeneous wholes. Clearly, this is hardly the case. The demarcation of "Asia" and the "West" is problematic in many ways. "Asia," as used in this essay, refers to East Asia and South Asia. The "West" refers generally to the United States and Europe. While it is obviously futile to descend into stereotypes, this essay does seek to highlight the fact that Asia is different in several ways, above and beyond dissimilar philosophies and the elusive term, culture.

First, what is tried and tested in the West has not always worked for Asia. For instance, during the Asian financial crisis in 1997, recommendations from the International Monetary Fund (IMF), which were imposed on the Asian countries as part of the conditions for the loans, did not alleviate the situation. Malaysia, which detracted from the recommendations, was among the first to recover. There were also suggestions that the IMF recommendations for maintaining high domestic interest rates, liberalizing the economy, and pegging currencies to the dollar were what triggered the financial crisis in the first place. In addition, most Asian economies have achieved the greatest level of growth under semi-authoritarian regimes, and examples include Taiwan, South Korea, Singapore, and China. While economic growth is not the best yardstick to measure the overall health of a nation, there are definitely indicators that the Western definition of democracy and its accompanying multiplier benefits have their limitations.

Second, the adage "It's the economy, stupid," so notably used by Bill Clinton during his 1992 presidential campaign, which has pretty much held up in the West, does not hold true for Asia. Asia has achieved rapid economic growth but not domestic political stability. From developed countries like Japan to developing countries like Thailand, from democracies like the Philippines to authoritarian regimes like China, most

Asian countries continue to be plagued by volatile domestic politics despite economic growth. Such instability can be partially attributed to the fact that Asia leans heavily toward elite governance, which is deeply embedded in Asian culture. It is virtually impossible for unknowns to make the mark. Political leaders are usually descendents of political pedigree or foreign-educated elites. The current political turmoil in Thailand is fundamentally a struggle between the rural class and the ruling elites, and Japan, which has appointed five Prime Ministers in four years, has only one Prime Minister, Junichiro Koizumi (notably a "non-blue blood") who has completed the full five-year term of office since 1972. This is a critical problem because if Asia does not achieve domestic stability, continued upheavals would certainly hamper economic growth.

Third, there is marked wealth disparity in Asian countries, without in-built mechanisms to handle the social ramifications or to redistribute wealth. According to an Asian Development Bank report in 2007, income inequality is on the rise in Asia and out of the 22 countries examined, 15 showed a rise in the difference in incomes of the rich and poor.[1] Asian countries have increasingly restive domestic populations as they make the transition from elation, as a result of economic growth, to disillusionment realizing that they are not going to benefit directly from the growth. And yet the Western solution of social safety nets and welfare systems might not work for Asia. Currently, only urban dwellers in China are covered under a very basic pension scheme and yet the pension system is already the single largest expenditure of the Chinese government. To include coverage of the remaining 900 million rural population (currently a trial scheme) would be a formidable task. Corruption and nepotism are also deeply embedded in many Asian societies.

Fourth, as many Asian countries have only recently (re)acquired their sovereignty, they guard it warily, and are apprehensive about any membership in organizations that requires them to cede sovereignty in name or in form. As a result, Asia is more inclined toward consensus-building, rather than applying pressure to influence behavior of other countries. Asia also prefers less committal and more noninterventionist modes of conflict resolution.

These characteristics of Asia necessitate a different paradigm in dealing with Asia's problems and charting its future development. In addition, Asia's newfound wealth affords it the resources and confidence to explore new modes of development and problem-solving. Decoupling is necessary for Asia to actualize its potential, and contribute proactively and constructively to the world. Decoupling would also allow Asian countries to have a more equal and productive relationship with their Western counterparts. However, the process of decoupling is fraught with several barriers.

A Delicate Balance

Decoupling is generally perceived negatively and it is indeed a delicate balance. The key is not to disengage, but to reduce reliance, diversify, and find Asia's niche and optimality. It is important not to alienate the West in the process. The rapid growth in intra-regional trade (which now accounts for more than fifty percent of trade in Asia according to the IMF), formation of regional organizations like ASEAN and its affiliated organizations, calls for the formation of an East Asian community, and the reduced reliance on foreign capital have triggered fears of the formation of an Asian bloc, designed to keep out the West.[2] This should not be the intent of Asia, and to fuel such a perception would be counter-productive—Asia needs the West and vice versa.

Evidently, the process of decoupling is not without baggage— many countries in Asia have a recent history of colonialism, and arguably went through a subsequent period of neo-colonialism where Westerns norms and standards were seen as the golden standard to emulate. Envisioning Asia striking out on its own, coming forth with alternative ways of global and domestic governance, economic models, and environmental management etc. takes imagination, determination, and confidence, without lapsing into complacency. Decoupling also should not be defined by aggression, the desire to claim an Asian era or to undo past "humiliation." Most importantly, decoupling entails a great degree of innovation, getting over inherent inertia, and the courage to challenge and change the status quo. As evident from the above, decoupling is both a physical and mental transition.

Forging a Path Forward

Despite these challenges, decoupling is desirable, achievable and necessary. This would entail several concurrent developments. First, as the latecomer to the game, Asia has the distinct advantage of leapfrogging and it should learn and adapt from the experience of the West in its development. It should also maximize the advantage to go even further by applying currently available technology and cutting-edge thinking to leapfrog the West, which remains hampered by investments and decisions made earlier in its own economic development cycle. This extends to all areas including infrastructure, environmental management, and education. Asia should build upon what has already been done by the West, but decouple by constantly incorporating, adapting, and reinventing.

Second, Asia should build and capitalize upon its own drivers and engines of growth. There are signs that this is slowly happening. Asian recovery from the recent crisis has been driven largely by the region's own economic demand and there has been a rebound in intra-regional trade. Although the region is less dependent on Western foreign capital than before, it is still reliant on export-led growth. Asia needs to cultivate an autonomous momentum of growth, by harnessing the rising purchasing power of the expanding middle class, continued investment in massive infrastructural development, as well as applying measures to expand intra-regional trade and investment. Although partially limited by the "spaghetti bowl effect," the proliferation of free trade agreements does mark Asia's commitment in the right direction. Asian countries should also continue to focus on confidence-building measures and foster interdependence, given the presence of fault lines within Asia due to territorial disputes, historical conflicts, clashing interests, and competition.

Third, Asia has to innovate on all fronts rather than merely benchmarking against the West or importing technology. There is strong consensus among economists that the biggest productivity gains stem from inventions. While Asia has been strong on investment-based growth founded on capital accumulation and imitation, it is very weak in innovation-based growth which stems from technological change and innovation. According to the World Intellectual Property Organization, while the United States is still the world's most inventive country, nearly 26 percent of all international patent applications last year came from Japan, South Korea and China. In addition, China registered a strong growth rate of 29.7 percent in the number of patents filed while the filing rate dropped by 11.4 percent in the United States and 11.2

percent in Germany in 2009.[3] This is a cogent indicator that Asia has the potential to push the frontiers of knowledge and innovation.

Lastly, Asia needs to perceive and carry out decoupling as a logical extension of its growth, and not a measure to break away from the West. This would be highly challenging, given the historical sensitivities and inherent competitive nature between Asia and the West, and the disparate agendas of the different Asian countries. To reap the maximum benefits from decoupling and avoid a backlash, Asia has to tread consistently and work on a collaborative approach with the West.

Global interdependence will always be a part of international relations, and the difference lies in a matter of degree. Decoupling would foster an independent but cooperative Asia which would be beneficial not just for the region, but for the world. Asia is well-poised to take advantage of the current upswing in its development and whether it makes the necessary leap to decouple from the West (and successfully manages Western sentiments in the process) would determine its growth path in the future.

Notes

1. "Inequality in Asia: Key Indicators 2007 Special Chapter Highlights." Asian Development Bank. 2007.

2. Gruenwald, P., Hori, M. "Intra-regional Trade Key to Asia's Export Boom." *IMF Survey Magazine*. February 6, 2008.

3. "International Patent Filings Dip in 2009 Amid Global Economic Downturn." World International Property Organization. Press release dated February 8, 2010.

Notes

Introduction

1. Calculations based on data from the U.S. Census Bureau international database, www.census.gov/ipc/www/idb/ (accessed May 20, 2011).

2. Simon Elegant, "China's Me Generation," TIME.com, last modified July 26, 2007, www.time.com/time/magazine/article/0,9171,1647228-1,00.html (accessed May 31, 2011).

3. Calculations based on data from World Development Indicators 2011, World Bank, http://data.worldbank.org/data-catalog/world-development-indicators (accessed May 26, 2011).

4. Euromonitor Global Market Research Blog, "Emerging Focus: Rising Middle Class in Emerging Markets," last modified March 29, 2010, http://blog .euromonitor.com/2010/03/emerging-focus-rising-middle-class-in-emerging-markets.html (accessed June 1, 2011).

5. Population Division of the Department of Economic and Social Affairs of the United Nations Secretariat, "World Population Prospects: The 2010 Revision," http://esa.un.org/unpd/wpp/index.htm (accessed May 5, 2011).

6. Asian Development Bank, "Asia Must Address Climate Change Impact on Water and Food," http://adb.org/Media/Articles/2011/13542-climate-change-impact-water-food/ (accessed May 3, 2011).

7. Asian Development Bank, "The World Bank's New Poverty Data: Implications for the Asian Development Bank," last modified November 2008,

179

www.adb.org/Documents/Presentations/New-Poverty-Estimates/Poverty-Data-Implications.pdf (accessed May 31, 2011).

8. Choe Sang-Hun, "In South Korea, Students Push Back," *New York Times*, last modified May 9, 2005, www.nytimes.com/2005/05/08/world/asia/08iht-korea.html (accessed May 27, 2011).

9. Karen Boncocan, "Youth Group Protests Education Budget Cuts," *Inquirer.net*, last modified September 29, 2010, http://newsinfo.inquirer.net/breakingnews/nation/view/20100929-295026/Youth-group-protests-education-budget-cuts (accessed May 27, 2011).

Chapter 1

1. Speech by U.S. President Barack Obama, Forsyth Tech, December 6, 2010, www.forsythtech.edu/president-obama/speech (accessed May 29, 2011).

2. UNESCO Institute for Statistics, "Enrollment Ratio Statistics," http://stats .uis.unesco.org/unesco/TableViewer/tableView.aspx?ReportId=182 (accessed June 16, 2011).

3. UNESCO Institute for Statistics, "School Life Expectancy Statistics," http://stats.uis.unesco.org/unesco/TableViewer/tableView.aspx?ReportId=185 (accessed June 16, 2011).

4. Population Division of the Department of Economic and Social Affairs of the United Nations Secretariat, "World Population Prospects: The 2010 Revision," http://esa.un.org/unpd/wpp/index.htm (accessed June 16, 2011).

5. UNESCO Institute for Statistics, November 23, 2010, http://stats.uis.unesco .org/unesco/ReportFolders/ReportFolders.aspx (accessed May 30, 2011).

6. United Nations, "The World's Women 2010: Key Findings for Asia and the Pacific," 2010, http://unstats.un.org/unsd/demographic/products/Worlds women/FactSheet2010.pdf (accessed May 30, 2011).

7. Michelle Riboud, Yevgeniya Savchenko, and Hong Tan, *The Knowledge Economy and Education and Training in South Asia* (Washington, D.C.: World Bank, 2007), xiv, http://siteresources.worldbank.org/INTINDIA/2132853-1191444019328/21497956/TheKnowledgeEconomyandEducationinSouth Asia.pdf (accessed May 31, 2011).

8. Diana Farrell and Andrew Grant, "Addressing China's Looming Talent Shortage," McKinsey & Company, October 2005, www.mckinsey.com/mgi/reports/pdfs/China_talent/ChinaPerspective.pdf (accessed May 16, 2011).

9. Riboud et al., xvi.

10. UNESCO Institute for Statistics, November 23, 2010, www.uis.unesco.org/Pages/default.aspx (accessed May 30, 2011).

11. Uttara Dukkipati, "South Asia Monitor: Higher Education in India: Sustaining Long-Term Growth?" Center for Strategic and International Studies, May 1, 2010, http://csis.org/publication/higher-education-india-sustaining-long-term-growth (accessed May 30, 2011).

12. Kee Beom Kim, "Youth Unemployment a Challenge in Asia and the Pacific," International Labor Organization, August 2010, www.ilo.org/wcmsp5/groups/public/—asia/—ro-bangkok/documents/article/wcms_144288.pdf (accessed May 30, 2011).

13. CCTV News, "Ant Group's New Year Wishes: Higher Income and Respect from Others," last modified February 24, 2010, www.cctv.com/english/special/news/20100224/105497.shtml (accessed May 31, 2011).

14. International Labor Organization, "Global Employment Trends for Youth," August 2010, www.ilo.org/wcmsp5/groups/public/—ed_emp/—emp_elm/—trends/documents/publication/wcms_143349.pdf (accessed June 7, 2011).

15. Quoted in Kishore Mahbubani, *The New Asian Hemisphere* (New York: Public Affairs, 2008), 60.

Chapter 2

1. Shaohua Chen and Martin Ravallion, "China Is Poorer than We Thought, But No Less Successful in the Fight against Poverty," World Bank Development Research Group, last modified May 2008, www-wds.worldbank.org/external/default/WDSContentServer/IW3P/IB/2008/05/19/000158349_20080519094812/Rendered/PDF/wps4621.pdf.

2. Angus Maddison, *Monitoring the World Economy 1820–1992* (Paris: Development Center of the Organization for Economic Co-operation and Development, 1995), 255.

3. Alan Wheatley, "Calculating the Coming Slowdown in China," *International Herald Tribune*, May 24, 2011.

4. Christopher Bodeen, "China BMW Collision Shows Anger vs. Rich," Associated Press, last modified April 6, 2004, http://forums.anandtech.com/showthread.php?t=1295085 (accessed May 30, 2011).

5. Asian Development Bank, "Key Indicators for Asia and the Pacific 2010," August 2010, 143, www.adb.org/documents/books/key_indicators/2010/pdf/Key-Indicators-2010.pdf.

6. MDG Monitor, www.mdgmonitor.org/map.cfm?goal=0&indicator=0&cd (accessed May 27, 2011).

7. Paul Tighe, "Economic Slump Raises Poverty Threat in Asia Pacific, UN Says," *Daily Mirror*, last modified October 18, 2010, http://print.dailymirror.lk/features/139-feature/24581.html (accessed May 27, 2010).

8. World Hunger Education Service, "2011 World Hunger and Poverty Facts and Statistics," www.worldhunger.org/articles/Learn/world%20hunger%20 facts%202002.htm (accessed May 30, 2011).

9. Wu Yiyao, "Rich Getting Richer, but Poor Becoming Resentful," *China Daily*, last modified December 10, 2009, www.chinadaily.com.cn/ china/2009-12/10/content_9151067.htm (accessed June 17, 2011).

10. "Thousands in India Protest High Food Prices," Reuters, last modified February 23, 2011, www.timesofoman.com/innercat.asp?detail=41774 (accessed May 30, 2011).

11. Michael Wines, "Truckers Protest, Adding to Chinese Fears of Unrest," *New York Times*, last modified April 22, 2011, www.nytimes.com/2011/04/23/ world/asia/23shanghai.html (accessed June 17, 2011).

12. International Monetary Fund, "World Economic Outlook Database April 2011," www.imf.org/external/pubs/ft/weo/2011/01/weodata/weorept.aspx? sy=1999&ey=2008&scsm=1&ssd=1&sort=country&ds=.&br=1&c=273&s= NGDP_RPCH&grp=0&a=&pr1.x=67&pr1.y=10 (accessed May 20, 2011).

13. Real-World Economics, "Gini Index for 17 Countries since WWII," last modified September 30, 2010, http://rwer.wordpress.com/2010/09/30/ graph-of-the-week-gini-index-for-17-countries-since-wwii/ (accessed May 30, 2011).

14. Asian Development Bank, "Fighting Poverty in Asia and the Pacific," April 2010, www.adb.org/Documents/Brochures/Corporate-Brochure/ Corporate-Brochure.pdf (accessed May 31, 2011).

15. UN Global Compact, "Global Initiative to Fight Human Trafficking," www .unglobalcompact.org/docs/issues_doc/labour/Forced_labour/HUMAN_ TRAFFICKING_-_THE_FACTS_-_final.pdf (accessed May 20, 2011).

16. World Bank, "Social Protection for a Changing India," last modified January 1, 2011, http://www-wds.worldbank.org/external/default/WDS ContentServer/WDSP/IB/2011/04/20/000333037_20110420235739/ Rendered/PDF/612750v20ESW0P11SP0Report0Volume0II.pdf (accessed June 17, 2011).

Anirban Bhaumik, "Sonia Rushes to Salvage MGNREGS," *Deccan Herald*, www.deccanherald.com/content/164386/sonia-rushes-salvage-mgnregs.html (accessed June 14, 2011).

17. "U.K. Orders Inquiry into Misuse of Sarva Shiksha Abhiyan Aid," *Business Standard*, www.business-standard.com/india/news/uk-orders- inquiry-into-misusesarva-shiksha-abhiyan-aid/398256/ (accessed June 14, 2011).

18. Grameen Danone Foods corporate website, www.danone.com/en/what- s-new/focus-4.html (accessed May 20, 2011).

Chapter 3

1. Population Division of the Department of Economic and Social Affairs of the United Nations Secretariat, "World Population Prospects: The 2010 Revision," http://esa.un.org/unpd/wpp/Excel-Data/population.htm (accessed June 16, 2011).

2. Ibid.

3. Ibid.

4. United Nations, "World Urbanization Prospects: The 2009 Revision," 11–12, http://esa.un.org/unpd/wup/Documents/WUP2009_Highlights_Final.pdf (accessed June 17, 2011).

5. United Nations, "China Now Home to One Quarter of World's Largest Cities," www.un.org/apps/news/story.asp?NewsID=34202&Cr=urban&Cr1 (accessed June 17, 2011).

6. Ministry of Housing and Urban Poverty Alleviation, Government of India, "Report of the Committee on Slum Statistics/Census," 21, last modified August 30, 2010, http://mhupa.gov.in/W_new/Slum_Report_NBO.pdf (accessed June 20, 2011).

7. "Has China Outgrown the One-Child Policy?" *Science*, Vol. 329, 3, last modified September 17, 2010, www.sciencenet.cn/upload/blog/file/2010/9/2010917535739887.pdf.

8. World Bank, "World Development Indicators Database," http://databank.worldbank.org/ddp/home.do?Step=12&id=4&CNO=2 (accessed June 20, 2011.

9. Samuel P. S. Ho, "Rural-Urban Imbalance in South Korea in the 1970s," *Asian Survey*, Vol. 19, No. 7, July 1979, www.jstor.org/pss/2643987.

10. National Portal of India, "Rural Development," last modified April 29, 2011, http://india.gov.in/sectors/rural/index.php.

11. Population Division of the Department of Economic and Social Affairs of the United Nations Secretariat, "World Population Prospects: The 2010 Revision," http://esa.un.org/unpd/wpp/index.htm (accessed June 16, 2011).

Chapter 4

1. Bettina Wassener, "Concern Over Environment Rises in Asia," *New York Times*, November 7, 2010, www.nytimes.com/2010/11/08/business/energy-environment/08green.html?pagewanted=1&_r=1 (accessed May 5, 2011).

2. William Gomes, "UN Sheikh Hasina in Copenhagen: Bangladesh, 'Most Vulnerable' to Climate Change," *AsiaNewsIT*, last modified December 17,

2009, www.asianews.it/news-en/Sheikh-Hasina-in-Copenhagen:-Bangladesh,-most-vulnerable-to-climate-change-17146.html (accessed April 6, 2011).

3. Ralph Jennings, "Shark Fin Out of Vogue among Young Asians," Reuters, last modified March 29, 2009, www.reuters.com/article/2009/03/30/us-asia-sharkfin-idUSTRE52T09M20090330 (accessed May 5, 2011).

4. "Budding Greens: A New Generation of Climate Activists," *The Economist*, last modified July 15, 2010, www.economist.com/node/16592268 (accessed May 5, 2011).

5. Christina Larson, "China's Emerging Environmental Movement," *Yale Environment 360*, last modified June 3, 2008, http://e360.yale.edu/feature/chinas_emerging_environmental_movement/2018/ (accessed May 5, 2011).

6. John Fien, David Yencken, and Helen Sykes (eds.), *Young People and the Environment: An Asia-Pacific Perspective* (Dordrecht, The Netherlands: Kluwer Academic Publishers, 2002), xiv, http://books.google.com.hk/books?id=zxo0gA_gdlwC&printsec=frontcover&hl=en#v=onepage&q&f=false (accessed May 5, 2011).

7. Food and Agriculture Organization of the United Nations, "The State of Food Insecurity in the World 2010," www.fao.org/docrep/013/i1683e/i1683e.pdf (accessed May 30, 2011).

8. Association for Responsible and Sustainable Investment in Asia (ASrIA), *Investing in Asia's Water Sector: A Turbulent Rush through Opening Floodgates* (Hong Kong: ASrIA, 2007), www.asria.org/publications/lib/ASrIA_water_report.pdf (accessed June 3, 2011).

9. For Food and Agriculture Organization: ibid. For UNICEF figures: *Progress for Children: A Report Card on Nutrition,* Number 4, May 2006 (New York: UNICEF, 2006), 2, www.unicef.org/progressforchildren/2006n4/files/PFC4_EN_8X11.pdf (accessed June 3, 2011).

Chapter 5

1. World Governance Index, "World Governance Indicator (Global Rankings in Descending Order)," January 2009, 76, www.world-governance.org/IMG/pdf_WGI_full_version_EN.pdf.

2. "Corruption Perceptions Index 2010," Transparency International, www.transparency.org/policy_research/surveys_indices/cpi/2010/results (accessed June 3, 2011).

Chapter 6

1. Patricia Justino, "Poverty and Violent Conflict: A Micro Level Perspective on the Causes and Duration of Warfare," MICROCON, January 2009, 2, www.microconflict.eu/publications/RWP6_PJ.pdf.

Chapter 7

1. *Ethnologue: Languages of the World*, 16th ed. (Dallas, TX: SIL International, 2009), www.ethnologue.com (accessed April 29, 2011).

2. U.S. Department of State, "Background Note: India," last modified July 14, 2010, www.state.gov/r/pa/ei/bgn/3454.htm (accessed April 29, 2011).

3. Masahiro Kawai and Ganeshan Wignaraja, Asian Development Bank, "Free Trade Agreements in East Asia: A Way toward Trade Liberalization?" May 2010, www.adb.org/documents/briefs/ADB-Briefs-2010-1-Free-Trade-Agreements.pdf (accessed May 20, 2011).

4. "Japan Remains Thailand's Largest Investor," *People's Daily* Online, last modified November 20, 2010, http://english.peopledaily.com.cn/90001/90 777/90851/7205365.html (accessed May 30, 2011); "China Denies Linking Cambodia Aid with Uighur Case," Reuters, last modified December 22, 2009, http://in.reuters.com/article/idINIndia-44914820091222 (accessed May 30, 2011); "China Tops Thailand as Biggest Investor in Myanmar," *Bloomberg Business Week*, February 21, 2011, www.businessweek.com/ap/financialnews/D9LH8K880.htm.

5. Andre Huang, "Rethinking Recruitment of Foreign Talent," *Taiwan Panorama*, last modified October 2008, www.taiwan-panorama.com/en/show_issue .php?id=2008109710019e.txt&table=2&cur_page=1&distype=text (accessed May 30, 2011).

6. "Money Means More to People since Financial Crisis: Poll," Reuters, February 22, 2010, www.reuters.com/article/2010/02/22/us-poll-money-idUSTRE61L2FK20100222?pageNumber=1 (accessed June 9, 2011).

About the Authors

Mark L. Clifford is executive director of the Hong Kong–based Asia Business Council. Before joining the Council in 2007, he spent 25 years in journalism, mostly in Asia. Clifford previously was editor-in-chief of the *South China Morning Post*; prior to that he was publisher and editor-in-chief of *The Standard* and had senior positions with *BusinessWeek* and the *Far Eastern Economic Review*. Clifford is the recipient of numerous prizes for his reporting, including the Overseas Press Club Award for best foreign business reporting for his coverage, as part of a *BusinessWeek* team, of the Asian financial crisis. He is an honors graduate of the University of California, Berkeley, and was a Walter Bagehot Fellow at Columbia University in 1986–1987. He is a member of the Council on Foreign Relations.

Janet Pau is program director of the Asia Business Council, where she leads research, publications, and member initiatives on a variety of topics related to Asia's economic development and competitiveness. Before joining the Council, Ms. Pau was manager at A.T. Kearney's Global Business Policy Council in Washington, DC, where she did strategy consulting projects for corporate and government clients around the world and co-authored a variety of the firm's flagship publications. She obtained a BA from Yale University and an MPP from Harvard University.

List of Contributors

Avish Acharya, 19, Nepal

Farooq Jamil Alvi, 29, Pakistan

Danica Elaine Ang, 22, the Philippines

Jan Brian Ano-os, 20, the Philippines

Abdullah Ansari, 24, Pakistan

Graeco Paul Antipasado, 25, the Philippines

Vibhor Bhardwaj, 23, India

Patrina Kaye N. Caceres, 22, the Philippines

Chim Chamroeun, 29, Cambodia

Hans Ching, 21, the Philippines

Sophie Choi, 22, South Korea

Dang Thi Phuong Thao, 29, Vietnam

Ronald Decina, 26, the Philippines

Reymart T. Deligero, 15, the Philippines

Zigfred Diaz, 31, the Philippines

Tenzin Dolma, 18, China

Francis Echon, 27, the Philippines

Siddharth Surendra Gadre, 22, India

Gemlyn George, 26, India

Saurov Ghosh, 29, India

Ian Teves Gonzales, 21, the Philippines

Sanjana Govindan-Jayadev Nair, 24, India

Anish Gupta, 26, India

Frederick A. Halcon, 31, the Philippines

Rohit Honawar, 29, India

Shreyans Jain, 20, India

Joseph James, 29, India

Ravleen Kaur, 16, India

Khan Asif Azad, 25, India

Khawaja Ali Zubair, 19, Pakistan

Kim Min-ji, 19, South Korea

Chandan Kumar, 28, India

Piyush Kumar, 25, India

Vineet Kumar, 21, India

Lee Meau Chyuan, 29, Malaysia

Liang Jianqiang, 26, China

Jeremy Lim, 18, Malaysia

Liu Mengyue, 27, China

Loh Su Hsing, 31, Singapore

Lưu Ngọc Thảo, 17, Vietnam

Marikit G. Manalang, 26, the Philippines

Ashwin Menon, 20, India

Reuben Andrew Muni, 27, the Philippines

S. Nagendra, 31, India

Yassif Nagim, 29, Malaysia

Kensuke Nakahara, 25, Japan

Aurodeep Nandi, 24, India

Sibtain Naqvi, 28, Pakistan

Tomoko Nishigori, 25, Japan

Benjamin Joshua Ong, 20, Singapore

Steve Or, 21, Hong Kong

Piyush Panigrahi, 21, India

Soyen Park, 25, South Korea

Rohit Pathak, 20, India

Pham Thuy Trang, 26, Vietnam

Poh Wei Leong, 29, Singapore

Vishwanath Praveen, 24, India

Buna Rizal Rachman, 22, Indonesia

Parkash Kumar Rajasekaran, 17, Malaysia

Rashmi Raman, 27, India

Omer Randhawa, 25, Pakistan

Vincent Bryan De Guia Salvador, 28, the Philippines

Kamanasish Sen, 26, India

Sudhansu Senapati, 29, India

Zofishan Shahid, 22, Pakistan

Aprakrita Shankar Narayanan, 16, India

Eeman Siddiqui-Malik, 27, Pakistan

Ankit Singh, 20, India

Sarabjit Singh, 26, India

Karishma Singh Ahluwalia, 31, India

Yushi Tanaka, 31, Japan

Tan Zi Xiang, 16, Singapore

Mariyam Thomas, 25, India

Akhilesh Variar, 23, India

Vincent Franklin Velasquez, 31, the Philippines

Wang Zhiqian, 27, China

Chomwan Weeraworawit, 29, Thailand

Megawati Wijaya, 30, Indonesia

Stevenson Q. Yu, 29, the Philippines

Sheraz Zaka, 24, Pakistan

Jesslyn Zeng, 15, Singapore

Zheng Zhonggui, 28, China

Index